MY OTHER HALF

MY OTHER HALF

A Memoir

JENNIFER KRAY

*To Mom and Dad
for never leaving my side.*

*To Dr. Baskaya, Solomon, and Big Mike
for believing in second chances.*

TABLE OF
CONTENTS

PREFACE

As the saying goes: God doesn't call the equipped, He equips the called. This book would not have come to be had it not been for the promptings of Mom's business partner, Kathy, and my neuroscience professor, Terry, who persevered in suggesting I write a book. As someone who wasn't motivated to read a chapter book cover to cover until her second year of high school and whose creative writing experience spanned one semester of her senior year, I felt I had no business writing a book.

But here we are.

More than seven years later, the following pages have come together to recount my experiences with suffering and how I found my identity in God as a result. I hope this book opens the door for more miracles to be seen and God's voice to be heard. Please enjoy following my journey in finding My Other Half.

PART I

CHAPTER
ONE

I WAS ON my tip toes, sliding my dollar bill to the bartender behind the lacquered wood counter. I wanted the bag of *Gardetto's* hanging from the chip stand. Saliva streamed along the insides of my cheeks, as I imagined the salty, garlic-flavored snack mix dissolving on my tongue; the doughy breadsticks and pretzels building on my teeth, leaving more to savor later. The checkered cereal squares had clumps of seasoning stuck in their little square holes I liked to suck on. But the bitter rye chips could stay in the bottom of the bag. Mom could eat those.

The shiny plastic bag crinkled as the bartender slid it across the counter. His pruned face looked hazy in the smoke trailing from the cigarettes of the two women at the bar who gasped at the sight of me. "Can we touch your hair?"

"Um," I paused as their mouths hung open. Mom was always with me whenever people asked. Orange slices and Maraschino cherries hugged the rims of their amber-colored cocktails. The smoke curling around them slithered in the same way it did around Mom and Dad whenever they smoked in the garage. "Let me ask my mom," I said.

I trotted across the carpeted floors in my rental bowling shoes that were one size too big. The only shoes in my size had Velcro straps, which I remembered the kids at school said were for babies. It was the larger shoes, with shoelaces, that cool kids wore, so I opted for the larger pair. They slipped off my heels as I leaned over the railing that separated the bar from the bowling lanes, where Mom was. I asked her if the two women at the bar could touch my hair. She straightened up in her chair and leaned back, trying to spot the women. She left my brother, Tom, at the score table and followed me back toward the bar.

She put her hand on my back and smiled at the women as we walked into their cloud of smoke. Mom introduced us as the women swiveled around on their green pleather bar stools, reaching out to pet my hair. My thick, frizzy waves puffed out several inches from my face. Mom's head held high as they gushed over its beauty and wished they could have just part of my hair to add to their own.

They were two of many strangers from my childhood who would get the chance to run their hands over my ever-widening locks. Among those who did and didn't know my name, I would come to be known as The Girl With The Hair.

The nickname stuck as well as Tom's did. Even though he was one year older than me, among his peers he would come to be known as Jenny's Brother. We lived on opposite ends of the spectrum. From his fair skin to my tan, his hobby of video-games to my hobby of sports, his straight A's to my straight C's, there wasn't much to agree on. While he went through his punk-gothic phase in middle school, I was belly-dancing and singing off key to the pop music blaring from my boom box in the foyer of our two-story home.

Every evening, Mom sat on the couch with a glass of wine as I begged her to make me famous. I wanted to be like the women on the covers of the magazines stacked on the end tables in our living room. They had straight, blonde hair and wore glamorous outfits. I had frizzy, brown hair and wore overalls.

Mom took me to dance classes, voice lessons, and modeling classes. I played small roles in community theater and tried several different instruments at school. As it turned out, I was moderately talented in the Arts and had little motivation to practice anything. Although neither of those truths dampened my hope of fame.

At home I stood on the wide base of our brick fireplace. The four can lights that lined the ceiling became my spotlights. My imagination put me in one of the skin-tight outfits covering the pop singer on the front cover of my favorite CD. Whoever was on the couch had to be my audience and clap when I was done performing. As I swayed my hips and glossed over the song lyrics I couldn't remember, I seldom noticed the crucifix sitting on the mantle above me; the one Dad brought home from one of his business trips to Israel. He got his faith from Grandma Kray, who was a devout Catholic. I saw her in him whenever he prayed at church.

Although he was notorious for his impatience and unreserved opinions, something about the way he closed his eyes and folded his hands made his humble connection with God obvious.

Mom, Tom, and I missed that appreciation for God at the time. Mom wasn't raised with religion and Tom may have already been leaning towards atheism. If I prayed, which I cannot recall doing, my prayers would be a plea for fame or for my school crush to like me back. A conversation which might be had with a genie is what my prayers would have been like. My mind ping-ponged from boys to clothes to hanging out with friends. I volunteered at the local rehab hospital and kept whatever sport I was in at the center of my attention. Anything but faith.

I reserved faith for praying at dinner time and attending Mass on Sunday mornings. In Mass, the readings were of no interest to me. I didn't know who the readers were talking about or why. The standing to sitting to kneeling to standing was annoying when I was already tired from waking up early on the weekend. I busied myself during Mass by studying the details of fabric in the shirt of the person sitting in front of me, gazing at my crush in the pew three rows up, or trying to rest my feet on the back of a pew without Dad noticing. I looked forward to each bout of singing.

I was in high spirits when eighth grade Confirmation came around. To be Confirmed meant I was officially an adult in the Church. As an adult, I could choose whether or not I attended Mass. I felt a sense of relief at my Confirmation, like I was earning a voucher or Get Out of Mass Free card. I slept in that next Sunday. Then, the one after that. Dad was the only one of us who kept going. Those mornings, after lumbering out of bed, the bottoms of my pajama pants dragged along our dog hair ridden kitchen floor. "Where's Dad?"

"At Church," Mom said, standing in her pink robe at the coffee maker.

I planted myself at the kitchen table with the easiest breakfast I could find. I scooped a spoonful of cereal into my mouth as Dad came walking through the door. He sat across from me as he laid open the *Chicago Tribune*.

"How was church?" I asked.

Even though he never complained, I felt guilty that he went to church alone. I joined him every once in a while, but otherwise waited to go as a family for Christmas and Easter.

The majority of my Catholic friends did the same, attending Mass only for the major holidays. Although our Religious Education classes must have taught us differently, applying only the seemingly positive and convenient lessons of the Bible to our moral compass was unanimous among my friends and me. The Bible was written so long ago, I doubted it could pertain to modern day. It wasn't like the people who wrote it knew what life would be like thousands of years later. Plus, the Bible was full of contradictions, violence, and suffering. What kind of God let that happen?

I stood firm in these opinions and doubts because my peers did. Saying or hearing Jesus' name outside of rote prayer, swearing, or Christmas or Easter Mass made me uneasy. On the occasion I heard one of the Bible-bangers in high school mention Jesus in a friendly or admirable way, I recoiled. While I had nothing against those people, it was as if their vulnerability to Jesus sparked my fight or flight response. So, I generally stayed away from them.

When I got to college, that fear lessened. My freshman roommate's friend invited us to the Christian fellowship events on campus. We attended some of the events for the sake of being polite, and in college, the walls you used to live behind growing up tend to break down. My roommate's friend introduced us to the other Jesus-lovers she knew. At their gatherings, all the guys talked to all the girls, but there was no flirting or gossiping. They had authentically calm, joyful demeanors which fascinated me. I couldn't pin-point what exactly made them different, but I wanted whatever it was. They talked about knowing Jesus, how they would hear him speaking to them. I didn't get it. How could they hear him? What did his voice sound like? They talked about Jesus speaking to their hearts, but how could words be in their heart?

I didn't gain any answers before transferring to the Catholic University where I pursued my master's degree in occupational therapy. Moving away from the Jesus-lovers made my intrigue in their lifestyle fade. The summer before school started, I found myself slipping into a relationship with a guy I barely knew.

Red, plastic cups and swaying college students filled the grassy courtyard of the townhouses surrounding us. He had a fake diamond stud pierced in one of his enormous ears and a cutoff t-shirt on. He was short with gangly arms. As we talked, I wasn't sure I could get past the size of his ears until he eyed the back of a blonde-haired volleyball girl walking by.

At the parties to follow, he flirted with other girls and asked me to "give him a moment" while he talked with them. The limited attention he gave me, made me want more. I wanted to date him. I wanted to date him for the sake of winning, for the sake of having what other girls no longer could.

As it turned out, I did them a favor. My relationship with this guy would destroy any backbone I might have had going into it.

TWO

W E DATED FOR two years. The end of our relationship was long-awaited by my peers and only came to be after a series of night-mares I had. In the nightmare, I would be at a gathering with family and friends. Their loud conversations would quiet to excited whispers as my gut turned, panicked by the sense that he was about to propose.

Or I would be in my wedding dress, panicked by the fact I was about to walk down the aisle to marry him. In the last moments of either dream, I was out of breath as I turned to Dad, saying, "I can't do this." Then, I woke up. I woke up yelling or crying, sometimes both, with the back of my neck and forehead drenched in sweat. After two weeks of these dreams, I couldn't stand it anymore. The next time I saw him I ended our relationship.

In the months leading up to this, I felt a nudge to return to Mass. The nostalgia of being at church comforted my otherwise lonely, lost soul. On the Sundays when God crossed my mind, I went to Mass. It was April of 2014 when my old freshman roommate's Christian friend sent me a care package after hearing about the break-up. I set the brown box on my desk as I ran the tip of my scissors across the packaging tape and pulled apart the cardboard flaps. Tissue paper crinkled as I pulled out a Feel Better card and a small book titled, *Devotional Journal*.

What was a devotional journal?

The pages fanned from the edge of my thumb. Each one was dated with a biblical passage to read. Beneath the passage was a prompt and blank space in which to write.

I started the journal that day, sparking my first conversation with Jesus. The hard shell I had encased him in suddenly broke. Jesus felt within reach. The journal spoke tenderly of him and how much he loved me. Many of my reflections were written from God's perspective, though I didn't write that way intentionally. His words would flood my mind. It was all I could do to keep up with my pen as phrases like, "I love you" and "you're beautiful the way you are," poured out of me. These entries triggered my newfound, unquenchable thirst to know Jesus.

In the meantime, I was engrossed with the calorie-counting I started earlier that year, in the thick of my toxic relationship. I didn't need to be tracking calories, but my doctor advised me to avoid processed foods to ease the chronic stomach pain I'd been having. Merely avoiding certain foods felt too subjective, so I eliminated them. Setting those boundaries made me want to set more, which is how I began restricting.

When I went home for Easter weekend Mom raised hell about the looks of my body. I weighed about one hundred pounds, twenty pounds lighter than she was used to seeing me. I didn't get what the big deal was. Her concern seemed blown out of proportion when she demanded I see a counselor. To get her to stop harping on me I agreed to go, which was how I ended up in Ali's office.

Ali was the school counselor on campus. In our first session, she asked if any stressful or major events had recently taken place.

I shrugged, "No." Then I remembered, "I recently broke-up with my boyfriend, but that's not stressful. It's the best thing that ever happened to me."

She was sitting in the gray armchair across from me, taking notes on her legal pad. She had a face full of freckles and a few intersecting wrinkles. Her expressions seldom varied. She was calm and, as I suspected, unimpressed with my story. I glanced at the width of my thighs, which were spread out flat like pancakes in my seat. My neck warmed and cheeks reddened as I thought about how stupid I looked for giving into Mom's concerns. My legs were still big. What if I wasn't skinny enough to be anorexic? Maybe there wasn't anything wrong with me.

I had one more session with Ali before summer break. The timing wasn't ideal, but I moved home to get a handle on what Ali and her nutritionist partner, Barb, agreed was "disordered eating." I was given a meal planning guide to help me gain weight and a healthy approach to eating. This meant reaching Barb's recommended daily servings.

The meal planning guide only fed the fire of my desperate need for control. In the evenings, I watched over Mom's shoulder while she cooked dinner. One night, she was standing in front of the stove as she slid a knife through a stick of butter and threw the greasy, square pad into the frying pan.

I gasped, "What are you doing?"

Streams of yellow liquid spread from the shrinking pad of butter, stretching across the pan as Mom's head tilted. "I'm making dinner," she said.

"I'm not going to eat it if you use butter. Butter's bad for you."

"Then what do you want me to use?"

"Olive oil," I said.

She turned off the burner and held the round skillet in the sink, under the faucet. Beads of grease scattered across the pan as if to dodge the rush of water.

"No," I said. My chest tightened. "You need a new one."

There could've been butter residue.

Metal crashed together as Mom pulled a new pan out of the cabinet and set it on the stove. She unscrewed a bottle of all-natural olive oil and waved it over the pan as the liquid drizzled across.

"No!" Tears welled in my eyes. "You have to measure it!"

Mom guessed, "It was a couple of tablespoons."

"But you didn't measure it. You don't *know* that," I said, as she threw a medley of chopped vegetables in the pan. How was I supposed to know how much fat I was consuming if she didn't measure it first? I pulled out my spiral notebook and put two tally marks next to "Fat," written on my daily nutrients list. Each tally mark represented one serving. Marking two tallies for the mystery amount of oil I'd be consuming at dinner seemed safe, a way to make room for error.

In the days to come, the unruly use of cooking spray made my body tense. The nutrition label claimed the contents had five calories per serving, but how could I know how many servings I used if it sprayed all over the pan? What if I sprayed more or less than five calories?

In the making of protein smoothies, I measured one cup of strawberries, which counted as one serving of fruit, and was marked in my notebook. The problem with measuring berries was they were different sizes and shapes. There were gaps between them, where small strawberries or strawberry slices could fit. I knew there were even more pockets of air in the measuring cup, where I couldn't see. Therefore, I didn't feel I had a true cup of berries. How would I know how many calories or servings I had if I couldn't measure the berries accurately?

I recorded every food I ate and for what meal. My nutrient list aligned with the margins of my notebook, reading Carbs, Fruit, Veg, Fat, Protein. I marked a tally next to the nutrient I consumed, whenever I had a serving of it. If I had half of a serving, I drew half of a tally mark. Even though Barb advised that I have ten servings of carbohydrates per day, if I surpassed seven tallies, I considered it a bad day. What if I met or exceeded the recommended intake and still wanted to eat more? What if I couldn't stop eating?

I avoided taking only a bite of something. That bite had calories. How could I measure a bite? On the rare occasion of doing so, I broke down the math the best I could. If a single cracker had ten calories and I ate a third of the cracker, I had 3.3 calories which I would round up to four as punishment for my spontaneity and lack of accuracy.

When I didn't have to eat, I sun-bathed in the backyard while writing in my devotional journal. God's words flooded my heart and I wrote all that I heard. I cried when phrases like, "you are mine," followed my pencil. I couldn't believe they were true.

When I moved back to campus for the fall semester, I brought Mom's old food scale to measure the number of ounces of protein I was eating so I could be more accurate with my tally marks. I liked to buy chicken tenders, but I didn't know whether to weigh them before or after I cooked them. Were they heavier and worth more tallies when raw? I brushed them with two tablespoons of barbecue sauce, 70 calories, and baked them to eat over a salad or single serving of rice.

I resumed my counseling sessions with Ali. I was proud of the way I was managing the meal planning guide. I consistently ate less than the ten recommended servings of carbohydrates. Seven servings felt safe. If I happened to eat less than seven, it was a pleasant surprise. When Ali asked how the meal planning was going, I responded with, "great" or "really well." To me, I was doing well. I wasn't exceeding the recommended servings and I was recording every food I ate. It didn't occur to my warped mind Ali would define doing well as following the actual meal plan. This and running would soon become topics of concern.

I was a long-distance runner. Average at best, but I took myself seriously. I woke-up at 5:25 a.m. every day except Sunday, which I deemed my day off. I timed every run and recorded the distance to make sure I was meeting the mileage I felt I needed to; anywhere between five and ten miles. Anything less didn't seem like enough. Each morning, as I ran from my apartment building to the main road leading toward the country, the sidewalk and trees would suddenly tilt to the side. A hazy film would bubble over my vision. I would shake my head to try snapping out of it. My fingers would brush the rough grooves in the sidewalk as I fought to keep my balance.

I always kept running. Every morning after my run, but before my shower, I weighed myself. I had to be naked and my hair had to be dry. I thought the weight of clothing or wet hair could make me heavier, skewing what I saw as my true weight.

I got a thrill the morning my scale's red digital numbers read ninety-nine. I had finally broken one hundred. I hadn't weighed under one hundred pounds since elementary school. In the mirror, I watched my finger slowly follow the waves of ribs extending from my sternum. If the bones in my chest seemed less visible from the day before, I was disappointed in myself. I feared I was gaining weight.

I didn't bring these details up in my sessions with Ali because they didn't seem alarming to me. I liked to see my body thinning. Ali asked me questions about the boyfriend I had, which confused me since our break-up had been such a positive aspect of my life. She wanted to know what my relationship with him had been like. The answer was easy; awful. My relationship with him was awful.

He and I barely left each other's sides, not because of how well we got along but because we didn't know how to be apart. If I hung out with my friends without him, would he be okay? Would he be lonely?

I felt nauseated telling Ali the way he wouldn't take no for an answer; how I often found myself lying in his bed when I said I didn't want to. With a flat tone of voice, he asked, Why?

I answered, Because.

Like a toddler, he responded, Because why?

Any sane woman with a single fiber of dignity would have left, but I couldn't. I was losing my sanity, and my dignity was already gone. Instead, I would sigh, roll my eyes, and say, Fine, to get him to shut up. While he used my body, I prayed for the Lord to intervene, for God to stop him. I would imagine being on the beach with the soft, but grainy sand beneath me. I would imagine the warmth of the sun and the mellow breeze coming off the waves. I would watch orange and pink hues illuminate the sky as the sun sank into the horizon. I dreamed of a paradise far away from the hell I was presently in.

He was a lot stronger than I was. I learned this when he pinned me against the fridge one afternoon. I don't have much memory beyond the moment itself, but I do recall us laughing and joking around beforehand. For whatever reason, he grabbed my wrists and pinned them above my head. My back flattened against the cool refrigerator door and my laugh faded when I told him to let go and he didn't. I tried pulling my arms down, but I couldn't budge them from his grip.

His legs were spread apart. The path to the door was clear. If I kicked him, I'd be able to run to the door in about three big steps. My purse was on the kitchen table, but I would leave it behind. I didn't want to waste time. I didn't want to give him any chance to grab me again. My right leg tensed as I eyed the fly of his jeans and suddenly, he let go.

Moments such as these, Ali pointed out, made my body seem to be a source of danger. My shrinking body felt less noticeable, less attractive, and therefore less violable. By controlling my weight, restricting calories, and over-exercising, I was trying to make up for the lack of control I had in my relationship. Ali said to write the phrase 'I Am Enough' on post-it notes and put them up throughout my apartment, where I would see them every day. She said the more I read it, the more I'd believe it. I did what she said, but struggled to trust the words I wrote.

The words I was connecting with were the ones written in my devotional journal. I was writing in my journal daily and going to Mass most Sundays, but I still wanted more. I started going to the Christian bookstore at least once a week to buy a new book about prayer. I turned down invitations to go out on the weekends so I could curl up in my apartment recliner and read instead. I was enamored with learning about God's desire to hear from me, to hear my prayers. Those books became my closest friends.

CHAPTER
THREE

T HE 9 A.M. Sunday Mass at our campus church became part of my weekly routine. If anyone asked me why, I didn't have much of an answer besides, "I just feel like I should." Although I had a seemingly irreversible habit of tuning out once the Homily began, being in the presence of the Mass felt restorative.

The Church had recently made changes to some of the words of the prayers spoken in the Mass. Therefore, most churchgoers read from the pamphlets provided, with the updated prayers in them. Even though the priest himself had to read from the pamphlet, doing so seemed like a weakness. I didn't want the surrounding parishioners to think I didn't have the prayer memorized—which I didn't—so I mumbled gibberish words to make it look like I had already mastered the prayers. I spoke loud enough so others could hear my voice, but soft enough so they couldn't hear the made-up words I was saying. I figured the movement of my lips would confirm for others I knew the prayer by heart, which I imagined would impress them and somehow make me better than them. Looking back, I am certain no one cared.

Like every other morning, I weighed myself before going to Mass. The lowest number that flashed before my feet was ninety-three pounds. I stared at the scale, thinking if I could just get to ninety- no, eighty-seven. If I could just get to eighty-seven pounds, then I would start regaining weight like Barb and Ali wanted me to.

But if I dropped down to eighty-seven, then I would want to lose a little more. If I got into the seventies, then I'd want to try for the sixties. I wished I could be zero, but no one could live at zero pounds. I needed my bones and insides in order to live, and those had to weigh something.

A chill raised the hair on my arms and drained the blood from my face as I realized the path I was on led to death. I had to start gaining weight.

Ali and Barb forbade me from running. My addiction to exercise was impeding my ability to gain weight. In hindsight, I would add that running kept my mind rigid. Manipulating the mileage and recording my times fed my need for control. When I learned of Ali and Barb's running-ban, I cried. If I hadn't exercised, I didn't feel worthy of food. How would my body burn calories if it hadn't worked hard enough to need them? Where would the calories go?

To eat without feeling like I earned the food was a daily struggle. One night I was curled up on the kitchen floor with my back against the cabinets. Tears streamed along the curves of my sunken-in cheeks, wetting the peanut butter stuck to the side of my lip. I pinched the corner of my half peanut butter and jelly sandwich. I knew I needed to eat it to have something for dinner. Yet, my rumbling stomach was drowning in the noise of my fear of becoming fat.

I wished for my roommate to come walking through the door. When she saw me crying over the sandwich, I could blurt out I was anorexic. I wouldn't have to keep concealing this secret. I wouldn't have to endure her suspicions anymore. But she didn't come. The door stayed closed and I stayed quiet.

I called Dad on my trips to the grocery store because he didn't tolerate the abstract-ness of mental illness. For example, in the years to come we would volunteer at a homeless shelter where there were several individuals suffering from mental illness. When I explained one man's apparent rudeness and impulsivity was due to his Schizophrenia, Dad called Bullshit.

I was standing in the cereal aisle at the grocery store one afternoon, eyeing a box of corn flakes. They had ten more calories per serving than the box of rice cereal beside it, but I really wanted the corn flakes. Grandma Kray used to serve us kids a bowl for breakfast on the weekends we went to visit her. She'd tilt the sugar-shaker over the tan, crunchy flakes, dusting them with the little, sweet crystals that made them taste better.

Even with that memory, I couldn't bring myself to grab the higher-calorie cereal. So, I called Dad.

"Hello?"

"Hey, I'm at the store right now," I said, turning the cereal boxes side by side to read him the labels. I told him how badly I wanted the corn flakes, but how I wasn't sure I should since they had more calories. What if I wanted to eat more than the serving size?

This was one of many grocery calls I made to Dad. He responded with answers like, "just eat it ... it's food, it's good for you ... everything is gonna kill you someday, might as well eat something you like." When I was still unsure, he added, "if you can't do it for yourself, do it for me."

I should have called him the day I was trying to pick out granola. I wanted the lowest calorie granola for the greatest serving size. The blueberry mix was 130 calories for a third of a cup, but the oats and honey mix was 110 calories for a fourth of a cup. What was the better granola? I flipped the nutrition labels around over and over, trying to remember what number of calories was in which box. I tried to calculate how many more calories the oats and honey mix would have if I had a third of a cup, compared to the blueberry mix. I wrestled with the math and my depleting memory for fifteen minutes before deciding to forgo the granola purchase because I couldn't figure out which had less calories.

Before bed each night, I knelt down on my carpeted floor and folded my hands against the flannel sheets covering my mattress. I buried my face in my arms and let my tears gush forth as I begged God for a miracle. I didn't care how or when it would come, but I knew I couldn't live this way anymore. Yet, I didn't have the strength to stop. When I laid in bed, my stomach growled. The hollowing sensation of hunger scraped along my insides as I rested my hand over my abdomen. "I'm so sorry," I whispered, feeling the warmth and softness of my skin as I cried myself to sleep. Still, I started the process over the next day by weighing myself, measuring out my meals, counting tally marks, and so on.

My mood swings were unpredictable. One day, before the running ban, I was working on a group project at our health sciences building. My classmates wanted to walk up to the second floor, where there was a sample of our given assignment. Our professor suggested we do this, but I refused. My legs were exhausted and sore from my run earlier that morning. I sharply insisted that seeing the sample was unnecessary; we could figure the project out on our own.

Their three faces drew a blank. Their jaws hung open and eyes shifted from one person to the other. After any one of my hormonal outbursts, a sudden awareness of how unreasonable I was being washed over me. This case was no different. I apologized and commanded our group to go to the second floor to see the project sample. When one classmate said not to worry about it, I retorted, "Nope. We're going." I waved my hand for them to come along as I walked toward the door.

My memory was also fading. One day, I asked a classmate how her weekend was. She rattled off a few things. I shuffled the papers on my desk and asked how her weekend was, again. She looked startled. As she answered me with the same answers, I realized I had asked her that same question moments before. I apologized and blamed my repetition on a lack of sleep.

I didn't see it at the time, but my health improved once I stopped running. I wasn't as tired and my mood swings had lessened. I wasn't pounding my emaciated joints on concrete every morning or waking up at dawn. The running-ban wasn't the answer to my recovery, but it was a crucial step forward.

It only took one example for Ali to change the trajectory of my disorder and give me a genuine motivation to eat. I was sitting on the couch in her office, where I always sat. She set her legal pad to the side and peered around the room. "Picture yourself at a bar," she said. "You're sitting on a bar stool, lined up with a row of women. Some women are whole, confident, accepting of themselves. Some women are broken and insecure."

I pictured myself sitting at the bar that most students swarmed on Friday nights, but instead of students they were women. Short, tall, skinny, overweight, older than me, younger than me.

"Guys like your ex-boyfriend come to the bar and prey on women who are broken. Those guys see the opportunity to manipulate and take advantage," she said. The thought of my ex-boyfriend's face, the thought of the musculature of his body, and the arrogance and manipulation that seeped from his lips made my stomach turn.

Ali went on, "The strong, genuine, respectful men-the kind you want to marry- come to the bar and leave those women alone. They sense their insecurity and know those women are not ready for relationships, not ready to be loved.

"If you stay on the road you're on," she said, "your future husband will pass you up because he sees a woman who's broken."

When our session ended, I burst out of her office. My backpack jumped side to side on my back as I barreled down the stairs to the lower level of the student center. I darted to the cafe, where I ordered a large, chocolate-peanut butter smoothie. I wasn't going to lose my future husband over this stupid eating disorder.

FOUR

I STOPPED AT the cafe at least three times a week to indulge in the large, chocolate-peanut butter smoothie. I drank these in addition to what I ate for breakfast and lunch those days. I continued using the meal planning guide, increasing my number of tally marks, but remaining hesitant to meet or exceed the recommended intake. Nonetheless, I was eating more and upped one jean size.

Weeks later, it was Thanksgiving break. I was lugging my duffle bag and backpack into the house when Mom dropped her cookie dough scooper in the kitchen to come give me a hug. Her short hair, stiffened with mousse, brushed my cheek as I wrapped my arms around the soft curves of her back. She said she had something for me as she walked to the opposite side of the counter and slipped me a small piece of paper. She said she ran into an old friend who has a son who is single. His name was Drew. He was working and living in the city. Since I was moving home to finish fieldwork for my last months of occupational therapy school, she thought maybe Drew and I could hang out and be friends. Her coy smile made it obvious she hoped Drew and I would be more than friends.

"Mom," I said, forgivingly. "This is the creepiest thing you've ever done. I got out of a crappy relationship earlier this year and I have no interest in dating anyone."

"What? Why not?"

"Because. Relationships always end in heartbreak. They start out with exciting, romantic feelings, and then they become serious, you get invested, and then they fall apart. I don't want to go through that again."

Still, she seemed excited, which made it hard to get the idea of Drew off my mind.

I was holding out for my future husband, so to get Drew out of my head I planned to call him that coming Tuesday, 10:30 a.m. He would be at work, I could leave a message, and he would never have to call me back.

It was perfect. We'd both be off the hook. In one of my school notebooks, I wrote down what I wanted to say so I didn't fumble over my words. I wanted to sound smooth, but not rehearsed. That Tuesday, I dialed his number. I was reviewing the script in my notebook, waiting for the call to go to voicemail when he answered the phone.

Who picks up the phone while they're at work?

We had our first date the day I got home for Christmas break. He said he would meet me at the train station after work that evening. He worked in an office on Michigan Ave, like a real, professional adult man, which made my former non-working boyfriend look like a goober. That boyfriend took me out to the bars with sticky floors and bathrooms you hoped you wouldn't have to use. Now, I was downtown in the hustle of successful adults and high-class restaurants and bars.

I was pacing in front of the tourist shop, trying to mellow the trembling of my legs and conceal the smile plastered across my face from passersby when my phone rang. Drew was at the train station.

"Hi!" I shouted into my phone in a surge of terror and excitement. He said he was by the cafe. My legs started trembling again as I stopped to look for him, but I saw no cafe. Then, he said he was by the escalators, but I didn't see anyone like him in the mob of businessmen filling the station. Most of them had slicked back hair and briefcases brushing the sides of their trench coats as they walked. I was describing the shops surrounding me when he said, "Turn around."

And there he was, tall with a classic crew-cut and flawlessly trimmed five o'clock shadow. My mouth opened but no words came out. He was my future husband, the one Ali said would pass me up if I continued down the path I was on. But here he was, right in front of me, not passing me by.

After dinner that night, we stopped in bars, passed through the same city streets over and over, doing anything we could to prolong the night and put off my train ride home. As the crisp, winter air invigorated the night, as our hands became intertwined, so too did our hearts. When we couldn't push back time any more than we already had, Drew hailed a taxi, handed the driver a twenty, and told me to let him know when I got home.

I nearly floated my way back through the station. I nestled in the corner of my seat on the train that night, leaned against the car's frosted window, and let our date run on replay in my mind all the way home.

The following weekend we met downtown for our second date, which was when he stopped me on the river walk to press his lips to mine for the first time. White puffs of air slipped from our mouths, mixing with the snowflakes falling around us. I slid my hands to the back of his neck as I would for many weekends to come. We perused the same city streets over and over like we did on our first date, trying to push back time. Instead of catching the train home, he asked if I wanted to stay the night. It felt early in our relationship to do so, but I wanted what he wanted. I couldn't risk losing a guy as good as Drew. So, I stayed the night.

I started fieldwork after the new year. I was finding my niche on the acute oncology floor at the hospital by Mom and Dad's house. Every Friday, I rushed out of work to drive into the city and spend the weekend with Drew. I felt like my life was coming together. I overcame my suffering, I was thinking about a future with Drew, and I would be graduated with my master's degree come June. I was putting together what I could see as a good, fulfilling future, but God allowed a different path to unfold.

PART II

CHAPTER
FIVE

February 28, 2015

I CUPPED MY hands around my mouth, watching the warmth of my breath slip through my fingers. I was wearing an extra pair of Dad's shooting gloves. The orange leather splayed across the back of my hand was soft and stained with dirt. The black mesh lining my palms did nothing in the way of capturing heat. The day's high was twelve degrees and although I anxiously awaited the coming of spring, I knew March's temperatures wouldn't be much warmer.

While we were at our lake house for the weekend, further north than home, I wondered what most Midwesterners do each winter: Why did we live here?

I followed Dad and his friend, Paul, through the aisles of broken-down corn stalks piled beneath a foot of snow. The frozen droplets glittered in the sun as I tromped by. With his shotgun slung in his arm, Dad yelled, "Jen, stay with us." Following them reminded me of the years Paul's daughter and I spent walking in their shadows through this same field. We carried the dead pheasants as they dropped from the sky.

Dad held out a floppy-headed rooster for one of us girls to take. Its eyes blinked softly once, twice, then closed. Its chest puffed one last time as it lost touch with the world. A red eye-mask decorated the rooster's face, contrasting the veil of velvety, emerald feathers over its head. A white strip circled its neck, separating the green feathers from the auburn ones cloaked over its body.

The wind carried expelled gun powder across my upper lip as I grabbed hold of the rooster's chest. The tips of my fingers warmed under its wing.

I liked stuffing the rooster in the back pouch of my blaze-orange vest. Its plump body warmed my lower back.

Dad's steel barrel snapped into place, triggering butterflies in my stomach as I longed to feel the same click reverberate through my hand.

Today, I was shooting with the boys for the first time.

I was still carrying the headache and anxiety I woke up with that morning. I figured I was dehydrated. While traveling, I only allow myself a few sips of water per hour to avoid the inconvenience of having to go to the bathroom. Dad says our three-and-a-half-hour car ride isn't a long enough drive to need a pit-stop.

My anxiety was from the anticipation of actually getting behind the barrel of a gun. I passed a day-long hunter's safety course back when I was fourteen. I remember practicing how to carry a shotgun when climbing over a fence and eyeing the blonde boy sitting next to his dad in class, hoping he had a crush on me, too.

Nine years later, I wasn't just following them in the field, I was hanging with them. I had Mom's winter boots on not because I didn't have my own, but because Dad insisted the rubber soles of her boots would hold up better than mine. I wore Tom's hand-me-down snow pants. They were tattered at the ankles and had a patch of duct tape Dad used to seal a tear in the right leg. If I could have worn more blaze-orange to better communicate I was a hunter and not a deer or animal to be shot at, I would've. Dad said wearing his hat, vest, and gloves was enough, though.

I caught up with them at the top of the hill. Dad waved his arm to the left as he called out, "Hup, this way Molly!" Her ears flapped in the wind while she ran zigzags through the field, paws hardly touching the ground. Her tongue hung out the side of her mouth, lips pulled back in a wide-mouthed grin as she swooped back towards us.

"Hunt 'em up, Mol!" I said, patting the spots ticked across her back. "Where're the birds at? Go get 'em!" She weaved around Dad and I, brushing against my side with her nose in the air. Her distraction peeved me given she was a better hunter than Paul's dog, Duke, who was working the field the way Molly should've been.

"Dad, what's wrong with her?"

"Just give her a chance," he said, patting her side. "Come on, Mol. Hunt' em up." At that she took off, barreling through the brush. She would have gotten the title, Master Hunter, after puppy school had we not spayed her already. Duke wasn't considered for that.

"Hey, she's got one!" Paul shouted, waving his hand in the air. "She's on point!"

Molly's nose was like an arrow pointing to a pile of combed-over field grass. Her liver and white-spotted coat shined in the sun, illuminating the bulk of muscle stacked in her back legs. She kept her head low to the ground with her left paw tucked tight to her chest.

Dad tip-toed toward Molly and glanced back at me. His voice turned low, "Okay, Jen. It's all you."

My heart pounded as I pointed my Christmas present toward the sky. A twenty-gauge, over-under. My first shotgun. Dad nudged his boot against the heap of grass, sending the hidden pheasant flying. Molly lifted her head, waiting for the pop of my gun.

My fingers moved in slow motion feeling for the curve of the trigger. I fought to get cheek to cheek with steel, trying to aim at the bird. The longer I fought, the lower the barrel pointed. My aim dropped to the horizon of barren trees. I rested the long neck of steel back in my arms. No one should shoot that low. The pheasant flew further and further into the sea of blue sky.

Then came a pop. Molly bolted, chasing after the pheasant free-falling from above. A mix of crisp air and gunpowder brushed my nostrils. Paul let his gun down. "Got him," he said, breaking the barrel and replacing the empty shells.

A wave of nausea pressed on the back of my throat. I prayed, telling the Lord it was freezing cold, I had a headache, and I felt like I was going to throw-up. And to please let us be done soon.

Another forty-five minutes went by before we made it back to Dad's truck. Its black body contrasted the backdrop of snow-covered oak trees. When I reached for the bed, I gasped as I remembered our family calendar. I told Dad, we should take a picture. Mom wanted us to take more photos for the calendar next year.

Making our family calendar was a Christmas tradition. I took over making it a couple years ago when Mom got tired of organizing pictures. Each winter, after several hours of scrounging for enough family photos, I vowed to take the always-needed more photos next year.

Dad's arm wrapped around my back as Molly stood between us. He handed his phone to Paul to take what would be the last photo of my Old Life.

Dad unloaded and stowed my gun in the bed of the truck. Molly and Duke budged their way through my legs as I climbed into the backseat. Their mouths were wide-open, teeth tapping against each other with playful growling noises bubbling up the backs of their throats. Molly's butt pinned me against the window, her back paws dug into my legs. I shoved back when their velvety ears perked at the rev of the truck engine. A mixture of gravel and snow crunched underneath our tires. The surrounding woods spun as we turned around.

I cradled my aching head as my arms and legs started cramping. Dad was notorious for speeding, yet the cornfields straddling the road home seemed to pass by slower than before. Couldn't we go any faster?

Duke stood with his front paws on the console, watching the houses in our neighborhood drift across the windshield. Dad pulled to the side of the road when we got to what we all called, the Buttercup Cottage. That was the name given in the real estate advertisement at the time and with its butter yellow siding, the name stuck.

With his hands full, Paul unclicked his seatbelt and elbowed-open the door. Goosebumps tickled my arms from the surge of cold air. He waved and promised to stop by later. I hunched forward at the turning of my stomach, hoping I didn't have the flu.

Dad pulled back onto the road, driving past our remaining neighbors' homes. Old Maggie's house was the one I wanted, the wood and stone-sided ranch. I hadn't met her or even seen her before, but everyone else had. So, I pretended I knew her too. Scary Cindy's was the next house, overgrown with evergreens and yew bushes. The summer after completing my school's drug awareness program in fifth grade, Cindy met me outside one night with a thin white stick hanging out the side of her lip. She held up a small carton, the size of Mom and Dad's smokes, asking if I wanted one. My heart raced as I repeated the line I learned from our fifth-grade sheriff, "No, I don't do drugs." Cindy scrunched her eyebrows, looking at me like I'd grown three heads. She pointed her flashlight to the picture of Spider-man shooting a web on the front of the carton. He was framed by the bold, yellow words Sugar Cane Sticks. I laughed nervously and still refused to take one.

The Rafferty's house was next to hers, another stone and wood-sided ranch. It was often just the parents who vacationed there. They had a large pontoon which seldom left the aluminum pier sticking out from their part of the lakefront. Molly liked to hunt for critters down by their shoreline and underneath their deck, which was next door to ours. We had a dusty blue, split-level ranch. My parents put the money down with their best friends from college the weekend of my fifth birthday.

In all those years we never bothered to seal our eroding driveway. My aching head bounced as Dad pulled into the bumpy, cracked drive. Molly smudged my window with her wet nose and hopped the console into the front seat. Dad's car keys chimed as he pulled them from the ignition, Molly whined at the sound of his door unlocking. She weaseled her way between his back and his seat, jumping out of the truck before he could. "Gah, Molly!" He grumbled.

Our chipped and fraying screen door was squeaky and made a crashing noise every time it closed, which made sneaking in past curfew tricky in my teenage years. As Dad followed me inside, clumps of snow melted off our boots squeaking between the linoleum floor and our rubber soles. My fingers moved in slow motion as they picked at my coat zipper.

I slipped off my jacket, tossing it along the carpeted steps at my feet. I grabbed the end of the railing, looking back at Dad as I stepped one boot up. "Can you please get some stuff out for lunch?"

"Yeah." He sniffed up the mucus dripping along the bottom of his nose as he walked into the kitchen.

I turned around and skipped the few steps it took to get upstairs. The bathroom was the first door on the left. It had a turquoise tub and toilet, iridescent tile flooring, and yellow walls. I flipped on the light, sending the fan into a deep, rickety hum. The fluorescent light mounted above the mirror drained my already paling skin. Dad's winter hat left my blonde and brown strands of hair standing like prairie grass on my head. I unraveled what was left of my French braid and reweaved handfuls of hair. Nearing the base of my skull, my left arm felt as if it was filled with lead. It grew so heavy I let it down to my side for a break.

I leaned sideways, bringing the end of my braid closer to my heavy hand. I grabbed the ends of my hair and tied it off with a hairband before my arm dropped back to my side. I thought of how weird this was, how it was kind of like what happens when people have strokes. When I stepped into the hallway, our morning hunt came to mind. I carried my shotgun in my left arm. I figured such a tired arm was what I got for carrying a gun around for two hours.

My stomach growled as I walked into the kitchen, grabbing the bowl of hummus and carrots Dad left on the counter for me. He was sitting in the big recliner, popping potato chips in his mouth. I pulled a wooden end table up to the small recliner, crunching on a carrot as I sat back. Dad and I stared out the picture window framing the village of ice-shacks on the lake. The white landscape of snow and ice radiated. Its light felt like needles darting into my eyes.

I shut them, turning away as my head exploded with pain. I peeked open enough to see the bottom corner of the couch. Its plaid, beige fabric and the white carpeting beneath it pierced my eyes. I hunched over, squeezing the bridge of my nose as if having a brain freeze.

Dad asked, "What's wrong?"

"My head. It's killing me," I said.

"Do you want some aspirin?"

"No, Mom gave me an Aleve before we left this morning." I slowly lifted my head, opening my eyes to the white, level-looped carpeting. Again, the daylight hitting its twisted fibers drilled my eyes. I buried my face in my lap and pinched my nose until my fingers started quivering. Was this what a migraine felt like? How did people live like this?

"Dad, I think I'm going to be sick." Tears began rolling down my cheeks.

"Honey, what's wrong?" Dad jumped out of his recliner and pulled my arms above my head. "Here, stand up," he said, pulling me to my feet.

My left arm dropped from his. My face crashed into his chest as my body collapsed to the ground. He knelt down, scooping my head and shoulders into his arms. "Jen, what's wrong?"

All I could do was stare at him. My heart was pounding. Half of my body felt suddenly dead. "Dad," I said, fighting to catch my breath, "call 911."

He shouted for Mom, "Jane!"

A faint "yeah" came from their bedroom upstairs.

"Jane! Call 911!"

CHAPTER
SIX

Mom rushed down the steps, through the kitchen. "What's going on?" Her eyes widened when she saw me lying on the floor in Dad's arms. There was a bit of hope in her voice when she asked, "Are you sure she's not just having a panic attack?"

Dad whipped his head around, "Call 911!"

Her face paled as she backed away and whispered, "Okay."

The dial tone whirred in the kitchen.

Maybe she was right. Maybe I was just having a panic attack.

The thought of calling the paramedics suddenly embarrassed me.

When I tried raising my heavy arm off the floor, my thumb and wrist twitched beside the brass stud on my jeans. My shoulder jumped in place.

It was moving again! I laughed nervously inside. Maybe I *was* just being dramatic.

I tried raising my arm again, but nothing happened. It laid in the fabric of my gray sleeve as if it wasn't mine. I had no sensation, no connection to it. When I tried raising my leg, my knee popped up. My foot turned inward, but then, nothing. It laid lifelessly on the floor just like my arm.

A lump swelled in the back of my throat. My jaw tightened, eyes grew glassy. I wished for Dad to hear my thoughts. I wanted to tell him I thought I was having a stroke. Then again, I was only twenty-three. How could I possibly be having a stroke? I studied the condition in my neuroscience course, but I couldn't recall young, healthy people having strokes.

Our screen door crashed open when the medics came through. Mom sprung towards them while Molly cowered by the foot of the recliner. I don't remember much about our conversation with the medics, but I do recall them asking about removing my boots and sweatshirt. The ER Doc would want them off, anyway. Dad helped grab my arms and legs, hoisting me onto the gurney. Layers of blankets were crisscrossed over my chest, tucked under my legs, and veiled over my head. Three large safety belts kept me snug on the gurney.

"Alright, here we go." The gurney raised. I was the closest to the ceiling I had ever been. How strange the kitchen looked from that height. The medics pulled me in the gurney into the hallway, leaving Mom, Dad, and Molly behind. Icy, winter air gushed through the doorway, trying to sneak into the folds of my blankets. I closed my eyes to the light bursting off the foot of snow covering our front yard.

The ambulance took us to the nearest emergency room, which was in the neighboring town where I ran my first half-marathon. I didn't look out the window, but I imagine the ambulance covered some of the same ground my feet did the year before.

Through the hospital entrance, my body shook as the gurney rolled across the tracks of the sliding door. We passed by a deserted nurse's station. Most of the lights were off and the surrounding patient rooms were vacant. The medics backed me into a room of nurses stretching latex gloves onto their hands. As one of the nurses kicked the gurney brakes on, another snapped an ID bracelet to my wrist.

"Honey, I'm going to take your jewelry off." She put the diamond earrings Dad gave me last Christmas into a disposable denture cup. She pulled at the ear piercing I got on a whim five weeks ago. I had an itch for a minor league-level act of rebellion one night. I picked up Paul's daughter and drove us to a tattoo parlor where they would pierce the pointy part of my ear called the tragus.

When we walked through the tattoo parlor doors, no one smiled. A group of teenage girls left the backroom in a fog of smoke, followed by a tall, thin man wearing a black, baggy t-shirt and pants adorned with chains. He walked to the front desk and called my name. I stood from the faux leather banquet hall chairs aligned by the entrance. His eyelashes were caked in glitter mascara. His blonde hair stretched outward as if he'd been electrocuted. Colorful tattoos covered his body, other than the patches of milky, virgin skin left on his face. He talked in a fast, high-pitched voice as if he'd inhaled helium. The only memory I kept of our conversation is his mention of a pet chihuahua.

Was it his or his friend's?

At some point in our conversation, he must've mentioned self-care instructions because I sprayed antiseptic on my ear religiously. Twice per day, every day for the weeks that followed. I had one more week to go.

What he failed to tell me, and I failed to ask, was how to remove the earring. Even though I had no other solution, I begged the nurse removing my jewelry to stop tugging on my piercing. The last thing I needed was my ear ripped off. She hurried out the door, recruiting a younger nurse to help. While the young nurse didn't wear a lot in the way of earrings, she untwisted the fake diamond stud and pulled the macaroni shaped earring without hardly touching me. Thank God.

Two other nurses shimmied my jeans down my hips, lifting my floppy leg from the table. They pulled off my shirt, unweaving my limp arm from its long sleeve. They threaded my hand through a lightly patterned hospital gown and draped its skirt over my knees.

A voice behind me urged, "Okay, let's take her." The gurney brakes clapped off and a breeze ran over my cheeks as we rushed down the hall. We turned into the last door on the left, meeting a giant donut shaped machine. Nurses and technicians surrounded the gurney, parking me alongside the machine and pulling taut the linen sheet beneath me. On three they hoisted me onto the hard plastic table that pinched my tailbone and other curves of my spine.

The older blonde nurse, with her north-woods accent said, "Okay dear, this will just take a few minutes." She spread a blanket over me, quickly folding down the edge bunched across my chest when she added, "Do your best not to move."

I closed my eyes, anguished by the pressure in my head. How could this be a stroke? There was no way.

The donut machine groaned as I focused on my breath. In one of my kinesiology courses, we spent a whole class talking about controlled breathing. In through the nose for a count of seven and out through pursed lips for a count of seven. As I laid in the donut machine, I did just that. In for seven, out for seven.

When the groaning stopped, technicians lifted me through the air with the taut linen sheet and back onto the gurney. They rolled me into the hallway. One nurse held onto the guard rail as she walked alongside me, saying Dr. Dhawan would read the CT scans and meet me in the room shortly. She and the other nurses backed me into my room where Mom and Dad were waiting for me.

The nurse asked what I would rate my pain level.

Could my pain have been any worse? I wanted to say ten, but if I said nine I could give myself room to increase my rating later, if need be. Still, I answered, "Ten."

Then, she asked me to smile for her. My gut plunged. She was looking for asymmetry in my face, one of the earliest signs of stroke. I smiled at the corner of the ceiling where the popcorn-tiles met the wall. Both corners of my lips pulled back to my cheeks, unwinding the tightness in my chest. She held up a small, laminated booklet and explained what I already knew. It was a flip-book, with common pictures and words to identify. She would show me a picture or word and I had to tell her what it was.

What if I had Aphasia? What if I couldn't read the words on the page? What if I couldn't say them?

She opened the book. Her finger teetered on the edge of its bold, Arial font. "What does this word say?"

The word was baseball. I parted my lips and when I heard "baseball" come from my mouth, my shoulders relaxed into the gurney. I continued my seven-count breathing.

I could read. I could do this. It would be okay. I could do this.

She laid the laminated book in my lap when Dr. Dhawan stepped into the doorway. The nurses quieted, standing with their backs against the walls. Dad held my hand while Mom rested hers on the curve of my shin. Dr. Dhawan planted his feet at the head of the room, clipboard tucked to his chest. "You're having a brain bleed."

CHAPTER
SEVEN

S HIT.

Mom rushed to Dr. Dhawan's side. As a nurse herself, she was fluent in the language of medicine. Through childhood, I didn't understand how people navigated life without a medical professional in their family. That, and a pick-up truck.

Mom's knowledge felt critical at times of sprained ankles, strep throat, and minor surgeries, like for wisdom teeth. Instead of staying in the hospital for my bout of pneumonia in the fourth grade, I slept in Mom and Dad's king sized bed for three weeks, hooked up to the IV bag Mom hung from the top drawer of her dresser. Every fall, I stood at the kitchen counter while she inoculated me with the flu shots she brought home from work.

Now, she was on the sidelines. Latex-lined hands reached above and below me. Sneakers scuffed in and out of the doorway. Questions bounced from wall to wall, "What's her pain rate?"

"Has anyone taken her?"

"Would you grab a few of those?"

My eyes stayed on Mom. She folded her arms and turned her head as she leaned towards Dr. Dhawan. His face was flat, emotionless. Her raspberry-painted lips—which turned pink every morning when she "put her face on," as she would say—whispered to him.

Dr. Dhawan lifted his clipboard, blocking my view of his words as he whispered back.

Mom gasped. Her eyes widened as she covered her mouth and stepped away. The lump pushed in the back of my throat, again. Tears welled in my eyes. I wanted to call out her name. What was going on?

Mom hurried to my bedside. She cupped her hands around mine and Dad's. Her eyes were glassy. "Oh, honey," she said as she tried to reassure me and convince herself, "it's going to be okay."

But I saw her. I saw her gasp, I saw her afraid. We had to stop this. We had to stop this now. Didn't they know? The longer we waited, the worse the bleed could get.

My throat tightened. I felt like I was breathing through a straw. The nurses seemed to be soundlessly tending my IV and dabbling through the room.

I began sobbing as I screamed inside for somebody to just do something, to help me!

Dr. Dhawan's hand waved in the air. He ran to my bedside yelling, "Stop! You have to stop crying! If you cry, you'll raise your blood pressure and make this bleed worse." My tears froze at the initial raise of his voice. He leaned into the guardrail beside me. "I am serious. You *cannot* cry."

My heart felt like it was fluttering against my chest. I felt sorry for the commotion, sorry for crying. He was right.

He stepped back to the foot of my bed, announcing, "We're going to have to fly you to get further care. We can send you to Appleton or Madison." He looked over at Mom, "Which do you prefer?"

Mom eyed the deadness of my left side and asked, "Where would you send your daughter?"

He looked down as if to skim the ground for answers, then shook his head. "They're both excellent hospitals."

Mom remained still, arms folded, waiting for him to choose. She knew no doctor wanted to answer the what would you do question, but she wasn't budging.

He looked down again, studying the toes of his black, leather shoes. "Madison," he said.

She nodded. "We'll go there."

"Okay. I'll call for the helicopter." Dr. Dhawan walked to the nurse's station sitting outside my patient room window. He reached over the desk, setting the office phone on the counter. He held out the receiver as he punched the numbered buttons.

Hanging above my patient room window was a clock with hands that seemed to be ticking at a glacial pace. Nurses shuffled around my room, fiddling with my IV or adjusting my blankets. They kept their gaze down as if to avoid eye contact with me, which I didn't mind. If we made eye contact, we would've had to acknowledge each other with a half-smile or a pointless question like, Doing okay?

Mom and Dad were leaning against the edge of the gurney, staring blankly. My throat was still tight, clenched around the lump swelling inside of it. I kept focus on breathing, blowing air through my pursed lips and sucking it back up through my nose. We were getting help. It would be okay.

Dr. Dhawan's loafers clopped down the hall before stopping in my doorway to announce the helicopter would arrive in twenty minutes.

My jaw dropped. Twenty minutes? Didn't they know we didn't have that kind of time?

He walked to my bedside, taking the one open space between the nurses crowding the gurney. He leaned into the railing, asking if I could smile for him.

I smiled at the same corner of the ceiling as I did before, but was irked by the sensation in my face. My right cheek felt heavy, flat. It wasn't moving. I closed my eyes as I sank deeper into the gurney. I was having a stroke.

My smile paled the faces of the nurses at my side. Their silence hung heavily in the air until one voice asked, "What is your pain rate?"

"Ten," I said, debating eleven or twelve.

The blonde nurse pulled my blankets up to my chin and folded them back across my chest. Dr. Dhawan and the other nurses filed out the door as she told me, "Now we have to wait for the helicopter. I'm going to step out of the room. I'll be back to check on you soon." She placed the call light in my lap. "Let us know if anything changes."

Changes? Like what kind of changes was she talking about?

She pressed her lips together and cast her eyes down as she stepped back. Her fingers lingered on my blanket as she walked towards the door.

No! She couldn't leave. We had to do something!

She was almost out the door when my view of the room shifted, pinwheeling to the left. I shouted, "Something's changing! Something's happening!" Tears burst from the corners of my eyes. My heart raced. I had crossed into the abyss of hysteria. While I didn't think of it then, this was the moment I realized my helplessness. What little control I had over my life not just in that moment, but in general. I depended on control to soothe my anxiety, to mask my lack of confidence, to make me feel productive. The foundation I spent ten-plus of my adolescent and adult years building shattered in a single morning.

The blonde nurse's ponytail whipped around. She hurried back to my bedside, asking what was wrong when a deeper voice bulldozed through hers. "Stop! Stop crying," Dr. Dhawan yelled as he rushed to my side. My tears stopped immediately, leaving channels of salt to crust on my cheeks. "You cannot afford to cry. You must stay calm."

Again, I felt sorry for crying and apologized profusely in my mind. My breath wavered as I sucked in the room's scent of sanitizer and latex through my nose and blew it out my pursed lips.

I had to breathe. It would be okay.

Dr. Dhawan eyed each person in the room. "The helicopter will be here soon," he said as his eyes landed on me.

"Okay." I whispered.

The room was quiet. Dr. Dhawan went back into the hallway. Mom kept a hold of my shin as she turned to talk with the nurse in lower, softer voices. Dad was leaning his elbows on the edge of the gurney. He slowly brushed the back of my hand along the white patch of whiskers in his graying goatee. His eyes were wide, staring off into space as he pressed his lips to the backs of my fingers.

My throat clenched to hold back building tears. I knew talking would unleash them all, but I couldn't cry. Dr. Dhawan said no. I couldn't cry.

Dad folded my hand into a fist, encasing it in his. He rested his lips on my knuckles, closing his eyes and squeezing my hand. I wanted to shout his name and tell him that this didn't feel right. We had to do something! This didn't feel like the way I was supposed to go.

Dad opened his eyes, studying the shape of my hand before returning to his far-off stare. I hoped he would somehow hear the thoughts surging through my mind. I didn't think this was God's plan. If it wasn't God's plan, we had to stop this. This was all wrong!

He blinked and met my gaze. My eyes clung to his. The tension in my throat softened just enough for me to whisper, "Dad." I waited through two more breaths to add, "just don't let me die."

"Oh, honey," he said. Tears welled in his eyes. His voice quivered as he shook his head. "You're not going to die."

How was this happening? I was so young, I hadn't even done anything yet. I hadn't even given to God.

A chill swept over my body.

Had I given enough to others?

CHAPTER

EIGHT

D r. Dhawan paced along the outside of my patient room window. He stopped to take a call at the nurse's station every few minutes, it seemed. A pod of nurses rushed from down the hall toward Dr. Dhawan. He nodded his head and came to my doorway. "The helicopter is here," he said.

The stripping of medical tape pulled my eyes to the nurse tending my IV. She clamped its tube shut and taped the cannula to my arm.

"Will I be okay?" I whispered.

She squatted down, meeting my eyes just above the bed rail. "Madison is an excellent hospital. There are doctors there that can help." She paused. Her mascara-coated eyelashes lowered before she promised, "I will pray for you."

I wanted to shout that I didn't need her prayers, I needed her to fix this!

A frizzy-haired woman came through the door, pulling an empty gurney behind her. Her ponytail hung halfway out of the collar of her puffy, red work-coat. Pushing the back of the gurney was a baby-faced, crew-cut, military boot-wearing man. They parked the gurney beside me. Metal guardrails crashed down to the sides. The linens beneath me pulled taut as the medics and nurses lifted me onto another gurney. They draped blankets across my body, tucked the ends beneath me, and fastened the safety belts over my chest and legs.

"Can at least one of us fly with her?" Mom asked the medic.

Her frizzy ponytail brushed her shoulder as she turned back. "No, I'm sorry. We have just enough room for her and the two of us. You'll have to meet us at the hospital."

Dad's grip tightened around my hand. In a low, steady voice he said, "You can pray Grandma's favorite prayer, the Hail Mary, or Grandpa's favorite prayer, the Our Father." He kissed my forehead as the medics rolled me toward the door.

It was happening. What if I didn't think I wanted to go? Why couldn't I just stay where I was? Leaving for further care made my brain bleed more real. If I stayed, maybe it would all go away.

"I love you. Everything will be okay," Dad said as I lost his grip.

Mom was standing beside the doorway. My mind felt empty. I impulsively held up my running watch and spare hair-tie. She grabbed them as our eyes locked onto each other. I gasped, Someone needed to tell them.

"Call Drew. Call Tom," I blurted just before the door frame cut us off.

Wintry air prowled the dim, empty hallway as we waited before the elevator. Its round light flashed and chimed when the silver doors slid open.

Pray. I needed to pray. Hail Mary or Our Father?

Metal clanked in the elevator walls as we rose to rooftop-level. The doors opened to a narrow hallway cluttered with cardboard boxes. The muffled chopping of propellers scraped along its yellowing walls. A blanket slipped around my head as we neared the exit door. "It's going to be cold out there," the female medic said.

The young, blonde man backed into the exit door, pushing it open as he pulled me with him. I squinted at the rays of sun stretching through the silky blue sky. The cold air slapped my cheek the same way it did out in the field that morning, mere hours ago. A black helicopter straddled the red medical cross painted on the rooftop. The medics' voices drowned in the propellers as they shouted commands to each other. My body jostled left to right as they loaded me into the helicopter. Buttons, switches, medical supplies decorated its narrow, coffin-like walls. The medics unfolded two seats from the wall and sat with their knees nearly tucked to their chests. The pressure in my head pushed out on my skull, making it feel like it was about to explode.

Pray, I needed to pray.

I closed my eyes as I recited Grandma's favorite prayer.

Hail Mary, full of grace, the Lord is with thee.

But my prayer stopped there. I didn't know any more of the words. How could I not have memorized this well-known prayer? I apologized to Grandma for not knowing the words and told Grandpa we were going with him. I prayed,

Our Father, who art in Heaven, hallowed be thy name. Thy kingdom come, thy will be done, on Earth as it is in Heaven. Give us this day, our daily bread, and forgive us our trespasses as we forgive those who trespass against us. And lead us not into temptation, but deliver us from evil. Our Father, who art in Heaven, hallowed be thy name. Thy kingdom come, thy will be done, on Earth as it is in Heaven. Give us this day, our daily bread, and forgive us our trespasses as we forgive those who trespass against us. And lead us not into temptation, but deliver us from evil. Our Father, who art in Heaven, hallowed be thy name. Thy kingdom come, thy will be done, on Earth as it is in Heaven. Give us this day, our daily bread, and forgive us our trespasses as we forgive those who trespass against us. And lead us not into temptation, but deliver us from evil ... but deliver us from evil?

My mind suddenly drew a blank.

What did it start with? What is that word? Kingdom come? No. Grandpa? No. Does it start with an F? Father? Our Father! Who Art in Heaven. Hallowed. Hallowed? Father?

As I lost my words, so too did I lose touch with the world.

CHAPTER
NINE

THE HUM OF water plugged my ears. I was gently bobbing in place, fully submerged in the midnight sky. The stars were all around me, like a sheath of golden freckles veiled over a dark, velvety abyss. The pain in my head was gone. I felt weightless. Something tugged at my side, a force, which slowly began pulling me along the sea of stars.

I prayed, This didn't feel right. I was only twenty-three, I had my whole life to give to Him still. This didn't feel like the way I was supposed to go.

Suddenly, the pull fell away. I was still. The stars shone like the snow-crystals glittering across the cornfields earlier that morning.

A crisp, soprano voice chimed in my ear, "You won't find the light."

What did she mean I wouldn't find the light? I had to find the light. That's what people were supposed to do.

I looked in every direction.

Where was it?

Another pull clutched my hips. It slowly began reeling me towards a star shining no more than the rest.

What if that wasn't it?

I looked around, scrambling to find a brighter light. The pull dragged me deeper into the midnight sky, accelerating its pace. Faster and faster the stars passed by.

I didn't know if that was it, I didn't know if that was the light. What if this wasn't right?

I begged for the pull to stop, but it only pulled me closer and closer until I was doused in a burst of light.

A sea of rolling clouds stretched beneath me and was layered on the horizon as far as I could see. Shades of pink and gold lined their wispy, cottony curves. To my right stood tall golden gates. Bars like harp strings ran up and down each one. The left gate was open part-way.

I sighed at the horizon, tired of fighting. "Fine. If this is what you want."

The crisp soprano voice returned. She whispered in my ear, "It's not time yet."

CHAPTER
TEN

March 2, 2015

THE ALUMINUM BLINDS in my hospital room windows were backlit with the morning light peering through my lashes. The drone of my bedside ventilator dragged through the air pumping in and out of my lungs. Its plastic tube pressed against the tips of my teeth, stretching my mouth into an oval shape. My body was still, as if cemented to the pillows propping up my limbs. Something was squeezing my lower legs. It would squeeze and relax, squeeze and relax, mashing my calf-meat like a deep tissue massage. The sound of running water flooded my ears, though no one was using the sink. A rubber feeding tube hung from my nose like a string of spaghetti, blending with the handful of tubes stemming from my head and neck. A turban of gauze, which Mom deemed my "hockey helmet," surrounded the deep, ongoing ache my head dwelled in.

Peeking around my hospital room door was a woman in scrubs. Her curly-haired bun crowned the top of her head. Her smile creased the only wrinkle on her face. She softly exclaimed, "I get to work with the miracle girl today!"

Miracle girl? That was sweet.

She walked to the edge of my bed and whispered, "Hi! I'm Natalie, I'll be your nurse today." She waved a barcode scanner over the plastic medical bracelet adorning my wrist. She said it was time for my medicine. I had three choices: Norco, Oxycodone, or Tylenol. She told me to blink once for No and twice for Yes. She slipped a stylus out of the scanner to punch in my order. "Would you like Norco for your pain today?"

Norco was a pretty serious drug. I blinked once.

"Oxycodone?"

People could get addicted to that stuff. No way was I taking that.

"Tylenol?" She asked.

I blinked twice.

She smiled and said she'd be right back.

I don't remember Natalie coming back, though I'm sure she did. Whenever a nurse brought my medicine, I didn't have to do anything. I didn't take a pill or drink a syrupy liquid. The nurse would come to my room, announce she had my medicine, and usually talk to Mom while she worked at my bedside. Months later, Mom explained I had a PICC line, a thin tube, in one of the veins in my neck that the nurses administered medicine through. This made sense since I was quadriplegic and intubated, although I never questioned it at the time.

My hospital room was shadowed by the darkness of night. The ventilator groaned its ongoing hum. My heart monitor beeped like the slow tick of a metronome. My flaccid body rested on the pillows supporting it as I begged Jesus to help me.

I felt trapped under a sheet of humidity as a rising heat scattered across my arms and legs. Red, digital numbers stared at me from the clock mounted on the ceiling. Two-twenty-eight a.m. several hours away from anyone regaining consciousness.

Mom's floppy, gray slippers peeked out of the layers of linen swaddling her body in the recliner. I wanted to shout, Mom, Dad wake-up!

Another wave of heat barreled down the back of my neck. My skin raged with a burning sensation. The hallway light glowed through the rectangular window in the door.

I needed help! Where was the nurse?

My chest tightened. Even though the ventilator was breathing for me, my breath felt shorter, further and further out of reach. I closed my eyes and begged Jesus to help, to wake someone, to do something!

Suddenly, I was watching Him. Among the infinite sea of wispy, rose-gold clouds, he was cradling my limp body in the nook of his arm. The sleeve of his cream-colored tunic pillowed the nape of my neck as my head hung backward. My long, sweat-soaked hair stretched towards the ground. He raised a tin pail, pouring cool water over my forehead. Streams of water trickled through my scalp, dissolving the heat.

Jesus raised the pail over and over, letting the water soothe my skin as I fell back to sleep.

CHAPTER
ELEVEN

March 3, 2015

MY EYELIDS BOBBED at the sunlight outlining the blinds, hanging like prison gates on my hospital room windows. Dad, Mom, Tom, and Drew were sitting on the couch opposite me, listening to the ventilator shriek, warning of my weakening breath.

"Jenny, you've got to keep breathing," Dad said.

I knew. I was trying. I imagined my lungs expanding like a pair of fleshy, greased balloons when the ventilator alarm sounded, again.

"Take a big breath in, you can do it," Dad said as he walked to my bedside.

A large silhouette filled the doorway. Big Mike. He wore navy blue scrubs, matching the rest of the nursing staff. His buzz cut, which he would tell me was the same length as the right half of my hair, nearly brushed the top of the door frame as he walked into my hospital room.

"Hey guys, how's it going?" He asked, "Can I get anything for ya?"

The room was quiet. The lights were off. "Nah," they said. "We're fine."

The ventilator shrieked, again, as a blow of air rushed through my lungs. Dad looked down and folded his arms across his chest. My body was still. My limbs felt like they were filled with lead.

"Okay," Big Mike clapped his hands as if huddling his team. "I'll tell you what, I'll leave it up to you." He motioned to them, "We can sit here, mope around in the dark and watch her sleep, breathing on the ventilator all day. Or we can open the blinds, let the light in, turn the radio on, and do something about this."

He walked to my bedside. A smile cracked from his right lip as he crouched down to meet me at eye-level. "What do ya say?"

I wanted to sleep.

But I had to get stronger.

Crows' feet stamped the corners of his eyes, which had an expectant look about them. He knew I was going to say, yes. How did he know me so well?

I blinked twice.

He nodded and rose to his feet. "Alright, let's do it!" He flipped the light switch, illuminating the fluorescent rectangles staggered across the ceiling. He pulled the cords hanging from the blinds, letting sunlight flood the room. Dad walked over to help. Tom and Drew stood from the couch as Mom stretched her arms.

I thought, Alright, let's do this.

CHAPTER
TWELVE

March 4, 2015

"HEY BEAUTIFUL," DREW said, taking a seat at my bedside. He leaned his elbows on the edge of my mattress and wove his fingers through mine. The corners of his lips gently pulled back as laugh lines creased the curves of his cheeks. His smile was all I needed to feel whole. I liked to graze my fingertips over the prickly hairs trimmed along his beard. I wanted to slide my thumb to the corner of his lips and press mine to his as I did mere days ago. His hair fell perfectly on his head. Maybe because he cut it himself. He couldn't stand the work of a hairdresser; always had to fix the mistakes they made once he got home.

The squeak of combat boots approached the other side of my hospital bed.

"Hey sister," Tom pulled up a chair, dropping his backpack to the floor. A black, thermal long-sleeve hugged his biceps. Boot-cut jeans covered the laces crisscrossing his shins and I didn't have to see to know a pocket-knife was clipped in the corner of his back pocket. A thick, auburn beard framed each of his words as he asked, "Remember my friend Nicole, the teacher?"

Nicole. The girl I nagged him to date, but he insisted was just a friend. I blinked twice.

He rustled through the front pocket of his backpack, "Well, her students, they're third-graders, ya know? Each of them made you a card. I thought I could read them to you." He pulled out a stack of three-by-fives. "Want to?"

My eyelashes fluttered. Of course I wanted to. It was so sweet.

He smirked as he untied them. "So, I briefly looked through the cards already and some of them are kind of bad."

Tom didn't care much for kids. They were expensive and needy.

He thumbed through the stack, pulling out a card with "an excessive amount of hearts and flowers," as he put it. He read the inside which said, Feel Better.

"Wow. How original," he said flatly and laid it on my lap.

His face scrunched at the sight of the next card. He turned the cover toward me as if to ask what the hell it was. A sea of blue scribbles drowned the doodles beneath them.

What was it?

He opened the inside, showing me the drawings. "I don't know what fish and hotdogs have to do with feeling better, but I'm sure Nicole gave him an A for effort." Drew and Tom chuckled. I was laughing too, but I wasn't sure they could tell. My face was flat, motionless.

Tom continued reading the cards. He guessed whatever figures the boys drew, from fire hydrants to stick-figure doctors. The girls tended to fill their cards with a combination of flowers, hearts, and rainbows. Tom called out the cards with backwards R's and S's and noted only the boys colored outside the lines.

A dull ache began pushing on the walls of my skull as my eyelids grew heavy. Any activity seemed to exhaust me. In the coming days, a couple of friends came to visit. When they played a romantic comedy for me, that would normally captivate my attention, I fell asleep before the opening credits were over.

Tom gathered the cards from my lap. "Why don't we finish reading these later?"

Yeah, later, I thought as my eyes shut and I dozed off to sleep.

Voices whispered. "She's still asleep ...."

"What time are they coming?"

"I'm going to take her blood pressure quick ...."

Soft voices danced around the room, pulling me out of my dream about speeding tickets and Bath and Body Works' lemon-scented soap. Slowly, I opened my eyes, adjusting to the brightness of the room.

"Hey Pinky, you're awake," Mom said as she walked to my bedside. She smiled at me the way a new mother smiled at her baby.

"Jane, do you ..." a nurse said, turning Mom's attention. She stepped back, conversing with the nurses by the window. "We can do that now or ..." they mumbled.

Hazy silhouettes stood throughout my room. Most things beyond the foot of my bed looked cloudy.

I wondered what I should do. Tom had offered to finish reading the cards ....

The hand gestures and head-nods filling Mom's conversation with the nurses gave little way for them to notice me.

Inside I piped up, Hey guys, Mom!

Her arms crossed as she continued in conversation.

How could I get her attention? My body was deadweight, but I needed to talk to Mom.

I batted my eyelashes, mimicking the cartoons on TV I watched growing up. They fluttered so fast, I got a headache.

"Hey, honey," Mom turned toward me. "Do you need something?"

Yes! Yes, I did.

"Are you in pain?"

No, I blinked once.

"Need to be repositioned?"

No.

"Do you need someone?"

Yes! I blinked twice.

"You need Dad?"

No.

"Drew?"

No.

"The nurse?"

No.

"Tom?"

Yes! My eyelashes fluttered.

"Do you want him to read to you?"

Yes! Yes, that was it.

Tom walked to my bedside. He pulled up the same chair from earlier and dropped his backpack in the same spot on the floor, against my bed. Reaching down, he said, "We can finish reading the cards or I brought a couple of books ...."

Books? What kind?

"Do you want to read the cards first?"

Nah. I blinked once.

"You want to read a book, then." Rummaging through his bag, he pulled out three books. "I brought *Harry Potter*,"

Meh.

"*Great Gatsby*?"

Not in the mood.

"*Bossypants*? I found it in your room."

I had finished the book a couple of weeks before, but still wanted the laugh it gave me.

My eyelashes fluttered as I blinked, Yes.

Tom thumbed the cream-colored pages, opening to the first chapter. "Okay, here we go," he said.

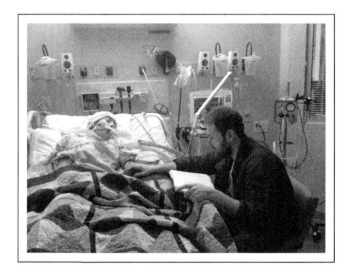

THIRTEEN

"HI JENNY, IT'S Dr. Luke." His voice was low and steady, "I'm here with Dr. Baskaya. Can you open your eyes for me?"

My eyelids slowly bobbed open to Dr. Luke's wavy, dark hair and handsome face, among the others surrounding my bedside.

What time was it?

The room was dark. Dr. Baskaya's accent rolled over my bedside as he said, "Here comes a bright light."

Was he Polish?

A single click preceded the burst of yellow light flooding my vision.

"Can you open a bit more?" Dr. Baskaya asked, spreading my eyebrow and lower lid further apart with his fingertips.

Didn't he know he could blind someone this way?

Darkness flashed as he switched eyes, flooding the other's visual field.

Another click cut off the head of light, leaving gray spots floating wherever I looked.

A soft, British accent sifted through the air. "Hi Jenny, it's Dr. Rose. Can you try wiggling your toes for me?"

I attempted pointing and flexing my toes. I could feel the sensation of their waving back and forth.

The amoeba of white coats surrounding her, whispered, "There one goes. Yep, I see it. Yeah."

Dr. Rose asked, "Can you try moving just your left?"

I waved my left toes, waiting to hear the whispers of excitement about my new movement, but there were none.

From school, I learned that sometimes recovering movement can be easier when both sides of the body try moving together, also known as bilateral coordination. Thus, I wiggled both my right and left toes.

Dr. Rose rested her hand on my right foot as she spoke, "I see your right toes are moving, but can you try moving your left for me?"

I was trying to move them. Didn't she know what bilateral coordination was?

Dr. Rose wrote on the folded papers from her pocket as she quieted the whispers of white coats behind her. "Thank you, Jenny, that is good," she said.

Dr. Luke summarized my present condition, as he did every morning. He reminded me I was on a ventilator to help with my breathing. He said they hoped to get me off of it as quickly as possible. The hallway's light peeked through the cracked door of my room, flickering across his face as workers walked by.

"Can you smile for me?" Dr. Baskaya asked, as he did every morning.

I smiled, feeling the weight of my flattened cheeks lie like a mask on my face.

"Can you give me a thumbs up?"

As I tried, my thumb felt like it was breaking out of concrete or packed sand. The sensation of my thumb raising was there, but only the tip of my thumb moved.

Dr. Luke's face dulled as he looked down at me. "This is going to be a long road," he said.

If we were talking more than two weeks; no, four weeks. If we were talking more than four weeks, they could count me out. I didn't have time for this. I had to be at fieldwork on Monday.

I was finishing my student internship at a hospital near Mom and Dad's. How would I get there, now? I couldn't drive. Would I treat my patients from my hospital bed?

I pictured my motionless body lying in my bed with a goniometer in hand. No way would my bed fit in the narrow space between my patient's bed and the wall. Maybe my bed could fit in front of the foot of theirs, but then my patient would be out of reach. How would this work? Would someone push me from room to room since I wouldn't be able to move?

The doctors and their white coated followers slid out the cracked door of my room as Mom leaned over my bedside. She adored Dr. Rose. Every morning Mom asked me, "Isn't Dr. Rose great? She is so beautiful ... and has that accent." Mom held my hand and stroked the side of my cheek, saying, "You're doing so well honey."

She set my hand down at my side and shuffled back to the recliner to sleep. The red digital numbers hanging from the ceiling read something like 5:21 a.m. My gut sank.

Couldn't it be morning yet?

I didn't like being the only one awake because I had no way to get anyone's attention. Once Mom closed her eyes, I started feeling warm. The heat rolled up my arms, curved around my neck, and over my head in the same way it did during the night. Inside, I shouted for Mom and Dad and begged Jesus to help me. My chest tightened and my breath seemed to get shorter and shorter.

I closed my eyes, finding myself back in the horizon of Heaven's rolling clouds. I watched Jesus cradle me in his arms as he did before, lifting the pail and letting the cool water run over my forehead, through my scalp. My mind hushed. My skin cooled as I fell back to sleep.

CHAPTER
FOURTEEN

March 5, 2015

AN ITCH CLIMBED the back of my tongue, nudging me awake. What was it?

Sunshine beamed through the open windows and across the bodies mingling in my hospital room. A silver pixie-cut framed the face of the woman leaning over my bed rail. "Hi Jenny, we're your Speech Team," she said as two more faces leaned over the opposite bedrail. She said they wanted to try out a few communication devices to see if they could give me the chance to talk some more. "We'll start with the most low-tech option."

She held up a black and white grid of the alphabet; six columns and five rows printed onto a sheet of computer paper and taped onto the back of a dry-erase board. She called it Charlie's Board because of the patient, named Charlie, who used it before.

"Let's practice once," she said, pointing to the board as she talked, "I'm going to point to each row first. Instead of blinking, why don't you try looking up for Yes and down for No. I think that'll be easier."

She was right.

"Look up when I point to the row that has the letter you want," she said. "Then, I will point to each letter in that row. Look up again once I point to the right letter. I'll write it on the dry-erase side to keep track."

Got it. I looked up as my throat tickled again.

What was it? It felt wiry. Was it hair? One of mine?

My feeding tube laced through my nose and ran down the back of my throat. What if a strand of hair was coiled around my feeding tube?

Ew! We needed to get this hair out.

Mom, Dad, Tom, and Drew huddled the speech team as they taught them how to use Charlie's Board. I practiced spelling my name while she wrote down each letter my eyes looked up to. Then, she flipped Charlie's Board to show me, "Jen," written in dry-erase marker on the backside.

One of her partners held out a black rectangular device to trade her for the board. She brought the new device to my face, asking if I could see its screen. It illuminated like a computer screen, piercing my eyes.

I looked up. I could see, but I wanted to shut my eyes. How could I ask her to please take the device away? Shutting my eyes seemed rude.

She tapped the device's keyboard and swiped its screen. Her words became white noise to me as the different colors, shapes, and words danced across the screen. The longer the light shined, the more I felt like my eyes were being gouged out of their sockets.

"Do you want to keep practicing with this device?"

I looked down. No, thank you.

"Would you like to go back to using Charlie's Board?"

I looked up.

She suggested Dad try asking if there was anything I wanted to say, if there was anything bothering me. He took the board and held it in front of his chest, asking, "Can you see the letters okay?"

I could.

"Is there anything hurting or bothering you?"

I looked up as the coiled hair pet the back of my tongue, again.

Dad pointed to the board, "Okay, let me know when I've got the right row." He wrote each of my chosen letters on the back of the board through a series of him pointing and me looking up, him pointing and me looking up until I finished spelling, D-O-B-H-O-F-F.

His forehead crinkled as he looked at what he wrote. "Dob-hoff?" His head jutted back as he turned the back of the board toward me. "I think I missed a letter. Is this what you meant to write?"

I looked up.

He studied the looks of the word, mumbling different pronunciations to himself, "Dobe-off ... do-be?"

It was pronounced dawb-hawf.

Mom looked over Dad's shoulder, "What does she need?"

"I don't know. I can't figure out what this means," he said, turning the board toward Mom. "This is what she spelled."

Mom raised an eyebrow and rolled her eyes. "Jim," she said, "it says, dobhoff. That's the name of her feeding tube." Mom tilted her head toward me and softened the tone of her voice, "Honey, is your feeding tube bothering you?"

I looked up.

The speech team leader leaned in, "Jane, using the board, ask Jenny what kind of pain she is in."

Mom raised the board for me to see. We worked through another series of pointing and looking up, pointing and looking up as I spelled, H-A-I-R.

Mom tilted her head and exchanged muffled words with the speech team. "Hair ... lines? Medication ... procedure?" The silver-haired woman stood with one arm crossed over her chest and one hand resting under her chin as she asked, "You think a hair is in your throat?"

No, I knew there was a hair in my throat. Still, I looked up.

Mom tried to reassure me, "Oh, that's just your feeding tube. It probably feels like there is a hair scratching your throat."

What? No. I could feel it!

The speech leader apologized, "I'm sorry you are uncomfortable. We'll let the doctors know."

"Maybe they can put in a G-tube," Mom suggested.

"That would be great, much more comfortable for her" she said, slinging a tote bag filled with communication devices. "Well, we are going to go and make Jenny her own spelling board, for tomorrow. That seems to be the most effective and what Jenny wants?" She raised an eyebrow toward me.

I looked up.

"Definitely. Thank you, so much," Mom said as she hugged the speech team.

"Of course. We'll be back tomorrow."

Mom held out Charlie's Board for the team to take back, but the speech leader hesitated. "Why don't you hang onto this for the night? You'll be able to practice and talk with Jen that way."

Mom smiled and nodded as she tucked the board to her chest. The coiled hair rubbed my throat as the speech team walked out the door. I couldn't make a sound, yet, with Charlie's board God was giving me a voice.

FIFTEEN

March 6, 2015

"Hi Jenny, my name is Shannon," the woman at my bedside said. She had a long-sleeve shirt layered beneath her blue scrubs, the same way I used to wear mine. She snapped a pair of latex gloves on, not quite covering the watch on her wrist. "I'm here to see you for physical therapy," she said.

"Hi Jenny," another voice chimed. "My name is Andrea. I'm here to see you for occupational therapy." She gestured to her left, "Shannon and I want to get you sitting at the edge of the bed. Does that sound okay?" Andrea's voice was sweet, quiet, and easy on my ears. Her strawberry-blonde waves rested on the shoulders of her floral cardigan.

Yeah, I wanted to get up!

Shannon reached across the bed and pulled back my sheets. She and Andrea lifted my arms and legs like a puppet, removing the pillows beneath them. Shannon's watch peeked out of the top of her glove. It was a sporty, digital watch like the one that accompanied me over miles of pavement and gravel. She must've been a runner, too.

Two nurses walked through the door, dragging a crane-like machine behind them. It was a Hoyer lift. I learned about them in school and used them in fieldwork to transfer the most dependent patients throughout their rooms. It would make getting my limp body to the edge of the bed easier on the four of them.

"Okay, here we go!" Shannon said.

The four of them moved with Shannon's words as she said, "Okay, gotta roll you on your side, here." Several hands pushed and pulled on my back and hips, lifted and held the lines and tubing extending from my body. "We're going to slide the sling underneath your back ...."

The monitor mounted above my bed sounded its alarm, freezing the bodies around me. "Oh, here," Andrea said. "Her pulse-ox slipped off." My pulse oximeter, the sensor taped to my finger to measure my oxygen level. These sensors seemed to always fall off my patients' hands, too. Each beep of my monitor sparked my memories of working with Will.

"Hi Will, it's Jen!" I would say, walking through my patient's door as I waved my latex gloved hand. My student hospital badge swung against my scrubs as I walked to his bedside, "Denise and I are here to get you sitting at the edge of the bed. How does that sound?"

He mouthed, "Okay".

"Great! We'll use the Hoyer lift." I rolled up our canvas sling and laid it along the side of his bed. "First, we'll get this underneath ya," I said, placing my hands under his hip and shoulder. What used to be a bulk of muscle along the back of his arm was now a bulk of sagging skin. Denise and I rolled Will side to side, spreading the sling beneath him and clipping each corner to the lift to get him out of the very thing that took his muscle away- this bed.

Moving the IV pole to her other side, Denise said, "I have his IV and the remote, do you have the other lines?"

As I gathered each one, I whispered, "Oxygen ... PICC ... Art line ..." and held the bunch above Will's head. "Yep, I got 'em. His cath-bag is on my side, too."

Denise would hold up the Hoyer lift's remote, saying, "Alright, here we go," just as Shannon did with the lift sitting beside my own hospital bed.

The sling beneath me inflated. It felt like what I imagined a cloud would feel like; plush and pillowy. The miniature crane lifted my body into the air. I was thinking about how nice the ride was when the ventilator tube shifted. It felt like four prongs of barbed wire were pulling on my throat from the inside out, which triggered an incessant, roaring cough. My arms curled toward my chest. My knees bent up to my waist. My face burned. I couldn't stop coughing. My chin jutted forward as I strained to take a breath in. The ventilator alarm sounded over and over.

Inside, I screamed for Jesus to help me. I couldn't breathe. His name reverberated through me as my convulsing body rocked the sling back and forth. The trach pinched the inside of my throat as it pulled and shifted.

I begged, Jesus, please help me!

Globs of phlegm were spewed from the corner of my mouth when I suddenly sucked in. It was no more air than what could pass through a straw. I coughed more and gasped again. When a full breath of air filled my lungs, the tension of my body melted. My skin started to cool.

Thank you, Jesus.

Glancing to her right, Shannon asked, "Do you have her trach tube?"

"Ye-ap, I got it." A pair of hands held up the excess tubing stemming from the ventilator. His fingers opened and closed, adjusting his grip as the hoyer lift turned. My trach tube shifted, again. A piercing pain tugged from the inside of my throat, setting off another coughing fit. The four of them raised their arms over heads and ducked down to their knees to work around each other, helping to guide my body and all of the lines coming out of it.

"We're going to lower you down," Shannon said as she climbed onto my bed, kneeling in the middle of the mattress. She tugged on a strap near my lower-back, steadying the sling as my bottom lowered to the edge of the bed. My back slumped into Shannon's body. Her hands straddled my temples, stabilizing my floppy head.

Andrea squatted in front of me, placing her hands on my knees. "I know this is a lot of work," she said. Silver sparks zipped across her face. The ache weighing on my body was bone deep. The room began to sway when she asked, "Are you doing okay?"

The thought of laying down sounded significantly better, but I had to get stronger.

I looked up. I'd be fine.

CHAPTER
SIXTEEN

March 8, 2015

A CREAKY NOISE chirped from the metal contraption towering over me, behind the cardiac chair I was propped-up in. The nurse had stuffed pillows under my arms and legs, on either side of my hips, and rolled one against my head to keep it upright.

An ongoing, aching pain compressed my body.

Andrea slid my left arm through a leather loop hanging from one of the cables. I looked like a marionette puppet waiting for the cable cords to pull my body back to life.

"So, I know this thing looks like a medieval torture device," she said, eyeing the cords running along the machine's side, "but I promise you, it's not."

My hand swayed back and forth, flopping at the wrist, as she cranked the cable until my arm raised to shoulder height. "Actually, you probably already know how this works, from your time in school," she said.

I looked up.

She turned to Mom and Dad as she pointed to the leather loop, saying, "This will take away the weight of her arm, making it easier for her to move on her own."

Andrea picked up what looked like a microphone. A purple, silicone dome topped the plastic cylinder forming the hand piece. The dome hummed, vibrating vigorously. "Try pulling your arm across your chest like you're reaching for the bedside," she said, tapping the rail of my empty bed sitting beside us.

I imagined reaching across my body, wrist cocked and fingers spread. She placed the vibration stick in the nook between my chest and armpit. "I'm putting a little vibration here to try waking up that muscle," she said.

The purple dome buzzed against my skin. I grunted inside, feeling as if I was dragging my arm through wet sand.

"There we go. Keep going! Pull, pull, pull!"

Imagining the movement of my arm felt confusing, too much to think about.

I grunted inside, again, trying to reach the bedrail. Why was moving so hard? It was as if my brain and body had never met. How did I do this before?

"Okay, take a rest" she said. She was giddy, smiling back at Mom and Dad. "Let's try that again! You're doing great."

CHAPTER
SEVENTEEN

March 10, 2015

MUMBLES ROLLED BETWEEN Mom and Big Mike who were standing shoulder to shoulder at my bedside. She hung her hand on my bed rail as she told him how I was a few months from graduating from occupational therapy school. Her words made me want to get back to my fieldwork rotation at the hospital, where my tennis shoes would squish across the shiny, tiled hallways leading to my next patient's room. I would curl my fingers into the cuff of the long-sleeved shirt layered under my scrubs. My folded sheets of patient names and room numbers would indent the front of my pocket. My scribbles about times of day, arrows, and abbreviations would frame that patient-list. A tube of chapstick and some colored pens would fill any extra space in my pocket.

During the last hour of what would come to be my last workday as a student, I stripped off my blue polyester gown and the latex gloves suctioned to my hands. I un-looped the medical mask from my ears and threw it in the garbage. Denise and I had been co-treating. We walked to the nurse's station, claiming two of the last open computers. My fingers grazed the keyboard as I submitted what would be my last note of documentation.

I was used to hearing my patients' ventilators beep, but now it was my own ventilator ringing beside me. Now I was the one in the hospital gown, glued to my bed, with a handful of cords stretching from my body. I felt buried in sand, trapped in my hospital bed.

Why did this happen to me? I wanted out, I just wanted to go home.

"Hey now," Big Mike said, tilting his head. "What's going on?"

I wanted to go home!

I sobbed inside, Just let me go home!

Mom folded her arms across her chest, "She's been a little sad lately. I think she misses home and school, just overwhelmed by all of this."

Big Mike grabbed the metal-framed chair behind him, taking a seat at my bedside. "Bad things happen to good people," he said and rested his elbow on the edge of my bed. "The drunk drivers, the rapists, the murderers; they deserve this. You did nothing to deserve this." He leaned in closer, "You are a good person."

He confessed to me the sudden end of his marriage, single fatherhood, his near-fatal fall into freezing waters, fighting through neuropathy to finish nursing school, and his ongoing comeback. I wasn't alone in my suffering. This hospital bed wasn't going to keep a hold of me, either. He concluded, "And you're going to get your ass back in OT school and be the best damn therapist that has ever walked this earth."

I looked up.

That evening, the sun sank into the city buildings outside my window. Patient-visitors lumbered through the hallways, zipping their jackets and rummaging through their pockets for car keys. Nurses sat at their stations, quietly typing medical notes. The bathroom light in my hospital room flipped off as Mom walked out in her fading heart-printed pajamas.

My stomach coiled as haystacks of blankets piled across the other side of my room. It was getting darker. What would the night bring? What if I needed them? I wouldn't be able to wake them up. They wouldn't know if I was in pain.

My head ached. It felt like a zip-tie was tightening around my skull. Pinching, pushing. What if I was having another stroke? I didn't want to die. I didn't want this to be happening.

"Hi honey," Mom whispered through the bed rail. "How are you?"

I looked down. I wasn't good. I thought I was having another stroke.

"The nurse just left, but she'll be back with your pain meds soon."

The imaginary zip-tie wound tighter around my head. How could this be happening?

A film of tears glossed Mom's eyes as she asked, "Are you sad right now?"

I looked up, Yes.

I didn't want this, any of this.

"You know what, honey, I started a blog to keep our family and friends updated on your progress. Everyone is praying for you. The whole Midwest is lit up for you."

I pictured the outline of the U.S. floating in the night sky with luminary candles scattered across the Great Plains, lit up for me. But I didn't need their prayers, I needed them to do something. I wanted to get out of this bed, I wanted to go home. I begged, Jesus, please.

CHAPTER
EIGHTEEN

March 11, 2015

MOM LIKED TO read me the comments made on the daily blog she wrote. One day, she was sitting next to my bed, balancing her computer in her lap. She leaned towards the bed rail. "There are a bunch of comments on your blog, want me to read them to you?"

I looked up.

She read a comment from my first-grade teacher, saying "I am so proud of your progress, keep fighting and stay strong. I am praying for you every day."

How did she find out this happened?

Mom swiped her finger up the screen. There was a comment from one of my classmates. Mom smiled as she tried holding back her laughter. She read, "Jen, I could always rely on you for a good laugh, and I thought you could use one today. Remember when we were in Lynn's class, when our group was being evaluated in the sim-lab and Hal's penis fell off?"

The ventilator shrieked. My diaphragm spasmed. My breath clashed with the air pumping through the tube in my throat. I was laughing.

Hal was the mannequin lying in the hospital bed in the simulation lab (sim-lab) at school. Three other classmates and I were in the midst of a lab-practical, which I found stressful only because I made it stressful. Even though being a student requires learning, which requires making mistakes, I was less focused on learning than I was performing. I stressed about doing my best, which I defined as not needing help and not making errors or my self-worth would be depleted.

I followed my classmates into the sim-lab. My eyes scanned the walls as I noted the sanitizer here, gloves there, blood pressure cuff by the bed. And there, in the bed, lay Hal. He was a talking mannequin given life by an electrical cord and Lynn's voice on the P.A system. He was waiting for us tucked under his covers with a creepy, yet pleasant smirk on his doll face.

He gave me the chills.

"Okay, Hal we're going to get you up and out of bed today," I said. "How does that sound?"

Lynn's voice came over the intercom while we stared at Hal, "Good."

My classmates, Chris, Chelsee, Katie, and I transferred Hal out of bed and into the lounge chair sitting in the corner. Chelsee took his blood pressure while I simulated brushing his teeth.

"Hal, our therapy-time is already up," Katie said. "Chris and I are going to help you get back to bed."

I stood on the opposite side of Hal's bed, waiting my turn to help while Katie and Chris transferred Hal from the lounge chair back to bed. My hands splayed across Hal's back to help keep him upright as they sat him on the edge of his mattress, when the sound of plastic tip-tapped across the floor.

Centered in one of the square tiles was his shiny, plastic penis.

My jaw dropped as we exchanged a series of panicked stares. What were we supposed to do? Pick it up? Put it in a kidney basin? Ask his pain-rate? Call the nurse?

Lynn's voice returned to the intercom, cueing our group to move along. Chris kicked Hal's penis to the corner of the room and we carried on.

Mom laughed as she said, "You never told me about that!"

I kept laughing and the ventilator kept beeping.

Mom cackled, "Jenny, you have to breathe!"

I couldn't!

My chest sporadically puffed up and down as the demise of Hal's genitals replayed in my mind. Mom swiped her finger across her computer screen, scrolling the page for more comments from her blog. As my breath regained rhythm, my chest felt heavy. I was exhausted from laughing my first, real laugh in my New Life.

Thank you, Katie.

CHAPTER
NINETEEN

March 12, 2015

"J EN!" MOM SAID, giddy at my bedside. "Your professor, Jon, is here! He made a device to help you communicate more easily." She side-stepped along my bed, making room for him to stand. The dim lighting made it hard to see, but I imagined Jon in his usual button-down flannel shirt and khakis. His beard highlighted the outdoorsy, wood shop-dwelling MacGyver that he was.

A woman, still bundled in her winter coat, stood at his side. "Jen, this is Helen," he said.

How was she wearing that? I felt like I was being roasted alive.

Jon sounded so professional. Since the start of school, I had wanted to see my professors at work, as therapists. I wondered what they said to their patients. How would they act? How did their work come so naturally?

"She helps me out with some of the assistive technology and will be working with us today," he said.

I didn't know he had an assistant.

Jon held up a small, purple-looking box. "I made this communication device with an Arduino microcontroller," he said. "It has a switch trigger. When you move your thumb close to the proximity sensor, it will detect your movement and play a recording that lists options for you to call the nurse or to spell out a word. A recording of the alphabet follows the spelling option. When you hear the letter you want to select, move your thumb. Then, the device will print out the letters you choose, like a receipt." He set the box at my side, wrapping my hand around it.

"You'll have to forgive me, my voice is the one recorded. So, you'll have to listen to me all day. I only had a week to do this."

What? He made this in a week?

A recording played from the little box in my hand, "A ... B ... C ..."

Jon leaned over my bedrail. "Once you hear the letter you want, swipe your thumb down."

"... F ... G ..."

I was waiting for H.

I groaned inside as I tried waving my thumb downward.

Come on, come on! Was it moving?

"H ..." the recording said.

Jon's eyes were fixed on my hand.

"I ... J ..."

I missed it.

"Jen, I see the tip of your thumb moving, but it's not enough for the sensor to pick up on. I made it as sensitive as I could, but if we need to adjust it, I'll have to take it back for the week."

Come on, thumb. I begged, Please, just work. I imagined my hand giving a thumbs up, the way Dr. Baskaya asked me every morning, as Jon's voice recording continued announcing the alphabet.

"L ... M ..." I had a perfect thumbs-up in my head. If it would just move up.

The device began making a printing noise.

"That's it!" Jon said. "Good job! I know it feels like a big stretch, but that's how far you need to move your thumb for the sensor to detect your movement."

The tip of my thumb waved up and down, selecting random letters as the paper printed out like that of a cash register.

"Once the recording runs back to the beginning, you'll have three categories to choose from, depending on what you want to say. There's an option to give yes-no answers, an option to use the alphabet to spell, or there's an option to call for the nurse."

"Here it goes," Jon said as the recording restarted. "Try choosing something else."

His voice buzzed from the speaker, "I want to spell ... I want to call the nurse ...."

That was it! Move, thumb, move! The former waving of my thumb filled my mind.

A siren whirred through my hospital room.

What was that?

Jon cheered, "Nice job! That's for calling the nurse."

It sounded like a prison alarm system. It just needed red, flashing lights.

Finally! I could get someone's attention.

As it turned out, Jon's device didn't last more than a day or two in my room. Mom and Dad, nurses and therapists; everyone was excited about my new ability to speak up, but my thumb wasn't moving enough for me to use the device efficiently. We returned to using Charlie's Board, which became my daily method of communication. Instead of relying on a device to get someone's attention, I had to rely on Jesus.

CHAPTER

TWENTY

March 14 , 2015

I WAS SITTING at the edge of the bed, slumped into nurse Natalie kneeling behind me. Her hands cupped my temples, keeping my head above my shoulders. My arms hung at my sides with my limp hands resting nowhere in particular. My body felt heavy, consumed by a deep, aching pain. Big Mike stood before me, grinning. He slid his hands to his knees as if to huddle with me when he asked, "Are you up for standing today?"

I looked up as quickly as I could. I hadn't stood on my feet in two weeks.

"Alright, let's do it," he said, clapping his hands together.

Big Mike bent over, wrapping his arms around me like a bear-hug as he counted down, "One ... two ...." On three, my chest glued to his. My feet flattened over the cool tile floor. The skirt of my hospital gown slipped back down to my knees. Plastic tubes and lines draped from my body. My legs quivered.

I was standing!

The ventilator finished pumping just one breath into my lungs before my knees buckled. Big Mike scooped me into his arms and laid me back in bed. My body was as exhausted as it was exhilarated.

I laughed inside. I was standing!

Big Mike beamed. "Awesome job! How did it feel?"

I looked up over and over. It felt amazing.

"We'll let you rest for a little bit," he said. "What can I help you with? Do you need your shoulders shifted? They look a little crooked."

I looked up.

He leveled my shoulders and smoothed the bedsheet beneath them. "Alright, now what about your hips? Are they uncomfortable?"

My hips felt okay.

"Knees?"

My knees felt lop-sided, but I didn't want him to have to do one more thing. It would be yet another favor to ask of him. I felt so needy in the ICU.

I looked down, I'd be fine.

He tilted his head and narrowed his eyes. "Don't you lie to me."

How did he know what I was thinking?

His voice became stern. "This is what I'm here for. If we have to do this all day just to get you comfortable, we'll do it," he said. "Now, would you like me to readjust your knees?"

I looked up.

My knees relaxed at his touch.

I didn't know Big Mike before my brain bleed, and now my body was hardly moving. I wasn't able to speak, yet he knew me. How? God was at work. He was in front of me. He was caring for me in my most vulnerable state, through the hands of Big Mike.

TWENTY-ONE

March 15, 2015

I WAS PROPPED up in the recliner next to my hospital bed when Dad's hands were kneading the ever-winding knots in my calves. A pillow rested under each one of my limbs and a pin-rolled bath towel kept my head upright. The tubes draping from my head and throat aligned with the others running down my arm. The recliner's seat felt like a rock under my bony bottom and although the pressure worsened as time went by, I had to stay out of bed to get stronger.

Mom and other silhouettes stood around my room, talking and watching me when Dad's hands stopped. "Hey Jen," he said, "wanna go on a run?"

I fluttered my lashes, looked up, and—per Big Mike's latest order—tried to move my lips to mouth, Yes.

Of course I wanted to go on a run.

Part of what made Dad an anomaly was how he looked like he could be a runner, too. Despite not having seen a gym in forty years, he was lean with chiseled muscles. He had the energy of a child, the kind that most adults longed for. Few nights passed without him having a bowl of ice cream before bed and a typical spring morning started out in the driveway. He would mount his bicycle in the same-sized Levi's he'd been wearing since college. He'd have his Iowa sweatshirt and ballcap on as he lit up a Marlboro Red before pushing on the bike pedal. He rode with a wispy wave of smoke trailing behind him. Its ashy nicotine coated my nose hairs.

I ran the same path he rode his bike on. If anyone knew where to take me on a run in the hospital, it was Dad. He pulled back the blanket draped over my legs and sat down. His hands clutched the soles of my feet like a pair of running shoes, pushing on them to bend my knees. One foot glided towards my hip while the other stretched towards him. Left, right, left, right, my feet ran through the air. "How many miles you wanna go?" Dad asked, "Five or six?"

Dad! I was probably out of shape. It had been weeks since I'd run. Two miles would be feasible. Then, we could go from there.

My lips rounded to say, Two.

"Two it is," he said. He moved my legs in even strides. I imagined drawing a big breath of thick, dewy summer air.

I would be shouting for Molly to heel while giving a quick tug to her leash as she lunged at ground squirrels scattering across the running path. When rays of sun broke through the canopy of waxy, green leaves on the trees, my head tilted back to soak in God's warmth. "There You are," I'd pray. Beads of sweat trickled along my forehead and dripped behind my ear. Gravel crunched under Molly's paws and the rubber grooves of my shoes.

Those warm rays of sun morphed back into one of my hospital room's fluorescent lights covered by a sheet of hazy dimpled glass. It shined on my knees popping in the air one after the other, kicking out toward Dad.

"How are you doin?" He asked, "Have we hit two yet?"

We probably had. I mouthed, Yes.

Dad laid my legs back down, across the foot of the recliner. He pinched the bottom seam of my hospital gown, pulling the bunched fabric back to my knees. He tucked my floppy feet under a blanket as the recliner seemingly sucked back onto my body. Air puffed through the blue tube, like a tentacle, hanging from my throat as the ventilator hummed.

I should've gone four or five.

Later that day, I was still propped up in the recliner as Andrea assisted my arm through a range of motions. Mom and Tom stood along the edge of my empty bed. Dad and Drew stood at my feet watching the sloth-paced movements of my body.

Andrea had been using the vibration stick to try waking up my muscles when she said, "Okay, you try." Her hands were in the air as if to show me she was unarmed. "I'm not going to touch you this time."

She shook her head, backing away from the recliner as she tucked the vibration stick to her chest. I imagined raising my arm like a toy soldier. The indent in the pillow beneath my hand puffed out as a five inch gap grew between my arm and the pillow, just before dropping back down. Andrea's eyes widened as she gasped. She covered her mouth and gushed, "Jen!"

I did it! I did it! I moved my arm!

Andrea's hands hardly hid the smile on her face.

I shouted inside, Look, I can do it again!

My arm raised and fell back to the pillow once more. Tears rolled over all of the smiles surrounding me.

Andrea gasped again. "Oh my goodness, I was not expecting that!" Her eyes turned glassy. She stepped back to my side, flicking on the vibration stick. "Think about bending your elbow," she said as she pressed its purple head to my bicep.

My loose skin jiggled, rippling like rings of water from the vibrating purple dome. She held my floppy wrist, brushing it along the side of my face as my arm bent.

She laid my arm back down, clicked off the vibration, and stepped back from the recliner. "Now you try," she said. My hand dangled from my wrist as I bent my elbow in slow-motion. The back of my hand neared the pair of black-framed readers resting on my face.

Andrea asked, "And what do we do with our glasses when we don't need them anymore?"

We would take them off.

I lowered my dangling fingers behind the right lens. My hand felt increasingly heavier as I hooked my fingers along the joint of the frame. I pulled my arm down, letting the weight of my hand slide the glasses to the tip of my nose. Another pull made the glasses tumble to my lap as my arm flopped down to my pillow.

Andrea cheered, "That was great! Let's keep going."

TWENTY-TWO

March 17, 2015

I HAD BEEN in the ICU for two and a half weeks when sherbet-colored rays of sun were melting into the horizon of my hospital room window. The ventilator was humming its regular tune beside me. I was sitting in the recliner with a myriad of pillows propping up my limbs and the trusty, pin-rolled towel that kept my head in place. It had been ten hours; a record for my length of time out of bed.

Mom was in her pajamas, sitting beside me and resting her arm next to mine when she fanned out a set of colorful magazines. "Okay, so we have *30+ Spring Palettes to Make Your Wedding Pop* ...." My friends and I gushed whenever we flipped through bridal magazines. We had been planning various versions of our hypothetical weddings since high school and never tired of dreaming-up pretend weddings for others.

"*Non-Stop Feuding* ...." A collage of photos decorated the cover, manipulated to mimic feuding between each celebrity family member. I would've been all over this before, but for some reason it wasn't enticing me.

"Or Kelly Clarkson, *I Can't Shed the Weight!*" She was walking on a sidewalk, looking down with her coffee in hand. Bold yellow letters surrounded her photo, spelling out the presumably fake quote, "I can't shed the weight!"

How was this type of magazine even allowed to be published? Last I knew, the woman just had a baby. But even if she hadn't ....

My appetite for gossip had spoiled.

I looked down. I didn't want to read any of them.

Mom reached to her side, picking up a legal pad and a permanent marker. The corner of her lip pulled back in a daring smile. "Or do you want to try writing?" The marker was wrapped in a red, cylindrical piece of foam. "Andrea built-up the marker to make it thicker, easier to hold," she said as she wrote through the air to demonstrate.

I looked up and mouthed, Yeah!

"Okay, let's put this here," she said, setting the legal pad on my lap, "and get your hand there." Mom wrapped my fingers in a fist around the marker, the way a toddler would. My grip loosened as the top of the marker teetered to the side. It rested along the curve of my thumb and finger. She held down the notepad fat-ways and cheered, "Alright, give it a go!"

My hand sat in the middle of the blue lines running along the page like prison bars. They intersected with the thin pink lines lying in its margin. The thought of swirling the wet, black ink to form letters, letting its sweet stinging smell climb into my nostrils fogged my mind. As if it was fused to the legal pad, my hand sat in place.

How did I do this before?

My eyes wandered to the grooves carved-out in the ceiling to avoid the sight of my hand.

I had to feel it. I imagined my wrist curling and stretching with each stroke of the pen.

What did it feel like? What did it feel like to make an H?

My whole arm moved in one big, clunky motion for each stroke of each letter. I reached forward, letting my hand slide to the top of the page. Black ink trailed behind my hand, slashing across the blue lines.

Now for the middle of the H.

My arm lifted and plopped on the left side of the page. The black ink cut across, curling a tail into the top corner.

And back down, I thought.

My arm lifted and plopped to the top right of the page. A short line jerked across the first diagonal. The butt of the marker leaned into the web space of my hand. My H looked like a pile of matchsticks or drunken tic-tac-toe.

Mom laughed as she flipped the paper to a new page. "Let's try again," she said and re-positioned my hand on the notepad.

I could do this.

I slid the marker to the left, dragging a crooked line down the page.

Whoops.

I drew a second crooked line from the top down, crossing with the first at its base.

Oops.

I pulled the ink from left to right to connect the middle, only to find another pile of matchsticks drawn on the page.

I laughed, wanting to tell her that this was pathetic. My chest puffed and deflated erratically as the ventilator began beeping.

She cackled as she tried to catch her breath. "Jen, you've got to breathe." She flipped to a new page and reset my hand. "Okay, okay. Try again," she said as the ventilator calmed.

I wanted to write something different this time.

My arm pulled down, dragging a short line of ink across the blue lines. I ....

My hand slid to the right to leave a little space. I drew another short vertical line and one horizontal. L .... My mind felt for the round belly of a circle. My eyes dawdled across the ceiling lights and slowly repelled down the wall.

How would I?

My shoulder jerked in short bursts to move my arm in a circle. O .... I pulled back and pushed forward. V ....

My mind continued to feel for the memory of the curved and angular bodies of each letter, the resistance of paper crossing the tip of a pen, and the pulse of my hand contracting and relaxing like a heartbeat for each stroke of ink.

The marker leaned into the web space of my thumb, again, when I finished writing. To my surprise, the words on the page were legible. I Love You.

"I love you too, honey," Mom smiled, letting the soft groan of the ventilator and the steady beeping of my heart monitor hang in the air for a moment. "Do you want to try writing Thank You, for Dr. Baskaya?"

I looked up.

I didn't know who he was, other than the man who Mom said saved my life. I didn't know exactly what she meant by that, either.

As Mom reset my hand on the paper, I wondered what a T felt like. My eyes veered toward the ceiling as my arm swung left to right, writing, T ... H ....

After U, my eyes dropped to the page. To my surprise again, the words were legible. None of the letters connected as they should, but the message was clear. Thank you.

Mom gave Dr. Baskaya the note the next morning. When she gave it to him, he looked hard at the paper. He stopped himself from folding it in half and passed it to the nurse beside him. I couldn't hear what they were saying and he didn't have much of an expression, from what I could see.

Did he like it?

Months later, Mom would tell me that when he read the note, he grew teary-eyed. He gave the note to the nurse to take to his desk immediately. He loved it.

TWENTY-THREE

March 18, 2015

I WAS BEING tucked into a gurney by the two medics in my hospital room. Mom walked over from loading up a bell-hop cart with bags and suitcases. "We'll see you soon honey," she said, kissing my forehead. "Love you!"

She was excited for change.

I had butterflies of equal excitement. The gurney wheels rattled as the medics rolled me out of my room. We followed the curve of the nurse's station, rolling through the ICU's hall of low lighting and dark-colored walls.

See ya never!

The long silver handles belted across the Exit doors clanked as they opened to a new hallway with rows of stark, fluorescent lighting and cream-colored walls. Healthcare workers' rubber soles squeaked as blood pressure machines passed in and out of patient rooms. Telephones screamed, ringing at the nursing desk.

A stiff-looking shirt collar bunched the skin beneath the buzz-cut hair of the medic at my feet. A light breeze brushed my cheeks as the quick pace of his boots made nurses and doctors step aside. "Take a left at G. The ambulance is outside of the west doors," his partner said.

He nodded. "Got it."

Why couldn't Mom or Dad have driven me? Dad could've been behind the wheel, Mom would have sat in the bucket seat, and I could've laid across the backseat with the ventilator hooked up in the trunk. Why couldn't we have just gone home?

The medic at my feet looked back. "It's about fifty degrees and sunny outside right now, gorgeous day," he said.

We got to go outside?

"Here we go!"

The glass doors slid open. A blast of cool, fresh air whirled across my cheeks and through the loose strands of hair waving from my turban of gauze.

I was outside! It was spring!

Sun beams stretched across the cloudless sky, warming my face. I sighed as I closed my eyes. I wanted to chug the crisp air like a glass of cold water.

I was thinking we should sit out here awhile when my body suddenly jostled left to right. The medics were already loading me into the back of the ambulance. My cheeks cooled as the sun disappeared, cut off by the ambulance ceiling. The smell of sanitizer and latex drowned out the fresh air.

One of the medics unfolded a seat from the wall by the foot of the gurney. He nodded his head curiously at me, flashing the OK symbol with his hand. His eyes shifted under his furrowed eyebrows. He looked hesitant, like he was holding his breath. It was as if he had freshly-learned skills and protocols reeling through his mind while he hoped I didn't actually need anything.

Yes, I mouthed. I didn't feel I had much of a choice. I tried giving a thumbs-up through the layers of blankets and safety straps pinning me to the gurney. He nodded his head and climbed into the bucket seat up front. Medical supplies clinked together as we navigated road construction at the base of the buildings formerly framed by my hospital windows.

The ambulance wheels thudded as we hit a pothole, jolting my body. The small of my back sank into the crease of the gurney, spreading a dull ache through my lower back.

This was gonna be a long trip.

Mounds of melting snow raced by the back window of the ambulance. The ocean of blue sky watched over the miles of concrete and muddy corn fields following along. A beat-up conversion van neared the bumper of the ambulance. The driver scratched his balding head as he looked from his rear-view mirror, over his shoulder and back to the rear view waiting to switch lanes.

Could he see me?

The dull ache in my lower back turned into a sharp, stabbing pain. I needed to scoot up.

I prayed, Jesus, help me.

The medical supplies crashed together as we hit another pothole. The gurney jolted, slumping my body further into the crease. A shredding pain tore through my lower back.

Jesus, help me!

The hesitant medic crawled from his bucket seat up front to the fold-down seat beside me.

I shouted inside, Help me!

He flashed the OK signal, tilting his head inquisitively.

I looked down and shaped my lips mouthing, No.

His expression flattened as he stared at me. He reached into the brown shopping bag Mom sent with me. He pulled out Charlie's Board, the grid of letters Dad would point at as I spelled out what I wanted to say. The medic held the board in front of his chest, quickly pointing from row to row.

He was moving too fast. His eyes jumped from me to the board and back. Before the letter could come into focus, his finger would move. His finger slid up the grid, pointing from column to column.

This wasn't how we did it.

His hand fell from the last column when he glanced to the front seat, then back at me with his dulled, dumb stare. He lowered Charlie's Board to his lap, trying to think of what to do. He flashed the OK sign at me, again.

Trying to communicate with him felt pointless. I sighed as I mouthed, Yeah, and looked away.

The brown bag crinkled as he buried Charlie's Board back where he found it. He crouched and climbed his way to the front seat. Miles of yellow-lined concrete continued reeling across the ambulance's back window.

I prayed, Oh Jesus, why? Please, take away my pain, please!

My spine felt like it was about to snap, but all I could do was lie still under the deadweight of my body, the layers of blankets, and the cross-body straps pinning me to the gurney.

My Jesus, please!

Three hours later, crisp air wafted from our bodies as we rolled through the tired beige wallpaper lining my new hospital's hallway. Oak-stained crown molding trailed the corners of the ceiling. We passed the nurses quietly moseying about the hall. The stabbing pain in my lower back fanned out from my spine, spreading up my back. I was screaming inside, begging for help as they backed me into my new room, across from the nurses station.

The ceiling spun as they parallel-parked the gurney alongside my new hospital bed. They unbuckled the gurney's straps, stripped the blankets off, and hoisted me over as my back pain melted away.

Thank you, Jesus.

The medics straightened out the blankets over my lap, unloaded the ventilator, and set Mom's brown shopping bag on the floor. A large woman came into the room in her pastel patterned scrub top and teal bottoms. A bun of corn rows was twisted atop her head. "Your mom just called, she'll be here in about twenty minutes," she said.

She followed the medics out of my room. Stillness loomed over the yellowing tile floors, the blank TV hanging from the ceiling, and the oversized day calendar on the wall. I wished Drew was with me, but he, like Dad and Tom, had gone back to work.

A clock hung above the bulletin board. Its black hands pointed to the bold one and two, reading 1:10 p.m. Its thin red hand ticked as it circled the corral of numbers.

Twenty more minutes.

After Mom arrived, my room became a revolving door for my new doctors to stop in and introduce themselves. Dr. O'Malley, my new physiatrist, was one of those who walked through my doorway donning a stethoscope, button-down shirt, and tie. He shook Mom's hand and stood before the foot of my bed. "The goal here is to get you off the ventilator," he said. "Tomorrow, you'll do a 12 hour breathing trial. Then, two days of 16 hour trials and finally, the 24 hour trial of independent breathing.

Once you pass that, we'll get you to inpatient rehabilitation as soon as we can."

Dr. O'Malley had smooth, cream-colored skin. His hair was blonde and his straight teeth gleamed when he smiled and nodded, goodbye. My big-bottomed nurse came back into my room with fresh linens and blankets tucked in her arms. "Here you go, Momma," she said, handing over the linens.

Mom spread the sheets over the cot sitting beside my hospital bed and nabbed an extra pillow from the cabinet above her. She leaned on my bedrail, yawning as she said, "It's already been such a big day." She smiled, "But I think we're in good hands."

Despite her hope, my stomach turned as I quickly drifted off to sleep.

CHAPTER
TWENTY-FOUR

March 19, 2015

EBONY CORNROWS POURED down the back of the respiratory therapist standing at my bedside. His name was Pax. A rubber band circled the bulk of braids gathered at the nape of his neck. His warm, tenor
voice rolled across my bedside every morning. "Okay, Jen," he said as he
crinkled a long, thin strip of plastic. He pulled a rubbery red tube from its
packaging. "First, we gotta do the suction."

Mom watched from the foot of my bed as Pax pressed his fingers to
my trach, unhooking the blue tube from my throat. "This will clear out
your airway," he said. "Take a big breath in." He flipped on the suction. It
whirred like a vacuum. At the peak of my breath, he fished the red tubing
through the plastic spout in my neck. Its rubbery body whipped around,
scraping the insides of my trachea.

My body flopped to the side, curling up like a roly-poly bug. My neck
stiffened. My chin jutted forward as I strained for a breath.

I shouted to Jesus. I needed air!

Pax slowly pulled the red tube from my throat, bringing cobwebs of
phlegm with it. A deep cough roared from my chest. Over and over.
Globs of phlegm spewed from my mouth onto my pillowcase as my body
thrashed back and forth. The muscles in my shoulders twisted and tightened. My head rolled off my pillow, onto the mattress.

I screamed inside, Jesus, help me!

My face burned. My veins were bulging and my head felt like it was
about to burst.

Jesus, help me! I begged again.

Peace radiated from Pax like mist rising from a waterfall. His calm gaze
cradled my sweltering, spasming body. My belly button nearly reached my
spine before a quick breath filled my lungs and shot out my mouth like a

bullet. My body kicked back, hurling forth another crackling cough. My arms bounced against each other as another gasp of air filled my lungs, easing the cranking in my neck. Slowly, a rhythm of breath formed. My body relaxed back to the mattress. My skin began to cool. The pressure in my head mellowed and my veins shrank back to size.

Pax placed his hands on either side of my face and laid my head back on my pillow. "Okay," he whispered, like a father comforting his baby. He attached my blue tube back to the plastic spout in my neck. "The ventilator is off, you can start breathing on your own," he smiled. "If you don't take a big enough breath, the ventilator will kick on to finish the breath for you."

Pax wadded up the suction wrappers and tossed them in the garbage as he neared the door. "I'll check on you in a bit," he said. Mom thanked him and waved as he left my room.

Twelve hours of breathing on my own. Twelve hours of my lungs expanding and squeezing. In and out, in and out.

TWENTY-FIVE

March 20, 2015

MY NEW OCCUPATIONAL and physical therapists, Holly and Beth, were standing with their therapy student at my bedside as I tried sliding my feet toward the edge of the bed. Mom watched from the chair in the corner of the room. My legs had lost the majority of their muscle and didn't look much thicker than the bones beneath them. They still felt stuck, buried in sand or cement, like they did in the ICU.

My right leg didn't slide but a few inches before Beth helped it move the rest of the way. Using my bed sheet as a sling, they scooped my floppy body to the edge of the bed for what we hoped would be five minutes. My back slumped into Beth, who was kneeling behind me. My hockey helmet of gauze had been removed, letting Beth's hands lay flat against each of my temples to keep my head upright. The therapy student squatted next to Holly who was kneeling at my feet. They were co-treating, like Denise and I used to do.

A wave of nausea swelled in the back of my throat. My stomach turned. I recited what became my edge-of-bed-mantra: Don't throw up, don't throw up, as Holly cheered, "You look great!"

An oxygen mask covered the opening in my trach. Pax had removed the blue ventilator tube earlier to kickstart my six-hour trial of breathing on my own, without the ventilator as backup. Holly pulled back the loose neck of my hospital gown that was revealing my jutting bones and shrunken breasts. Sweat beads dampened the skin along my hairline as I continued reciting my mantra, Don't throw up, don't throw up.

Holly put her hands on my knees and asked, "Are you doin' okay? Still feeling good?"

A wispy fog began clouding her face and all that was around her. Silver stars started zipping across the frothy clouds. Could I still vomit with a trach tube in?

I looked at the bits of space still showing her face as I mouthed, Yes.

"Alright, we've been sitting up for almost five minutes now," she said, looking at her stopwatch. "Let's get you back in bed so you can rest a bit."

The student gathered the extra slack of oxygen tubing. Beth cradled my head and laid my shoulders back down to my mattress as she scooted off my bed. Holly lifted my legs, setting them along the foot of my bed.

As soon as my head laid down, the fog dissipated. My stomach settled. Holly and Beth stuffed a pillow under each of my arms and pin-rolled a towel to prop up my head. They scanned my bed, checking for twisted or misplaced lines. Holly set the call light under my hand. Beth pulled my covers taut.

"Okay, dear, we'll see you tomorrow!" Holly waved as they walked out the door.

CHAPTER
TWENTY-SIX

March 21, 2015

D REW WAS STANDING behind my bed, weaving the half head of hair I still had left from surgery into a braid. He YouTube'd how to braid before driving out from the city to visit for the day. Like Dad and Tom, he had returned to his job, leaving most of our time together for the weekends.

He sprayed the bottle of detangler Tom dropped off after a challenging exchange of lip-reading. Tom had been at my bedside, smirking as my mind began to piece itself together after a trip of Oxycodone eased the pain of my muscle spasms. Drew had mentioned the numerous knots in my hair and when Tom asked me if there was anything he could get me from home, I mouthed, Detangler.

"What?"

Detangler.

"Chapstick?"

Detangler, I mouthed again.

He squinted, studying the movement of my half-paralyzed lips.

"You want to watch football?"

What? No. Context clues, Tom. We were talking about hair.

I mouthed, Bottle.

It was a red bottle of kids' detangling hair spray, sitting in my bathroom cabinet at home.

"Something about bananas ...," he cackled.

I rolled my eyes. Why would I be talking about fruit on the topic of hair?

Bottle, I mouthed again.

"Bottle?"

Yes!

By the grace of God, Tom finished lip-reading my request for the red bottle sitting in my bathroom at home.

That was the bottle Drew sprayed over my head, brushing through my long hair and stopping at every tangle that caught the brush. "Sorry Jen," he said as he picked apart the knots.

Mom set aside her computer and leaned over my bedside. She looked at the oxygen mask covering the open spout in my trach. Her nail glossed the rash growing on the front of my neck. It was the same oval shape as the oxygen mask itself and itched so bad it burned. I lifted my hand to my neck, letting my fingers dangle in front of the rash, still too weak to scratch my skin. I was 12 hours into breathing without the ventilator, which turned into 16 hours. Dr. Fitzpatrick thought I was doing so well that I could keep breathing and shave a day off my vent-weaning protocol.

Mom glanced toward the door and smiled. She said, "I think there's someone here to see you."

A man dressed in a suit and tie stood in my doorway.

It was Dad!

He had been traveling for days, touching base with Mom over the phone. "Hey honey!" He came to my bedside, leaned over the bedrail, and kissed my forehead. He slipped off his sport coat and tossed it on the back of a chair. He rolled up his sleeves, cracking a smile as he asked, "Wanna go for a run?"

That evening Dad and Drew left, leaving Mom to be the one leaning against my bedrail. "Honey," she sang. Her face was still blurry as I was just starting to come out of the medicated stupor my afternoon nurse put me in. "Jen," she said, "you look stoned."

I was lying lifelessly, like usual, in my hospital bed. The swaying of my room was slowing when I decided I couldn't stand the icy, cold pack freezing my lower back anymore.

I mouthed to Mom, The nurses put an ice pack beneath me.

"Why?" Mom asked.

I mouthed, Pressure sores.

"You don't have any pressure sores."

Yes I do, I mouthed, I heard them talking about it today.

Mom stared at my half-open eyelids.

I mouthed, Roll me on my side and take out the ice pack. I'm cold.

Mom smirked as she pulled down my sheets. She bent one of my legs over the other, and rolled me onto my side as the cold sensation slipped under my bottom.

"I don't see anything," she said, laying me back down.

How could she not see it? It was an ice pack.

Look again, I mouthed.

Mom laughed as she rolled my bony body on its side again.

The ice pack must have slipped underneath me, where she somehow couldn't see it.

As she held her hands against the back of my hip and shoulder, the coolness of the pack slipped under my bottom again. She laid me back down and said, "There is no ice pack, Jen."

You had got to be kidding me.

My lips moved furiously as I mouthed, The ice pack slides underneath me every time you roll me to the side. You have to get it out.

For a third time, Mom rolled me over to find no ice pack.

I mouthed, Look under me once more, where the ice pack slips *every* time.

"There is no ice pack," she laughed.

Her laugh lines became clearer and my room regained its stillness as I mouthed, Yes there is, I can feel it!

She glanced across the room and began to keel over. She pointed to a tube sitting on the counter. "Jenny, they put Bengay on you. It's menthol cream that's making you cold. They probably used the cream to prevent pressure sores."

I glared at the plastic tube. It all made sense. There was no ice pack. I couldn't recall any conversation with a nurse, but rather just mumbling about pressure sores.

Mom was right.

CHAPTER
TWENTY-SEVEN

March 22, 2015

MOM WAS STANDING in the dark, unwinding the aluminum blinds hanging in my hallway window. Lab coat and scrub-layered bodies raced through the tunnel of fluorescent lights. "Code blue, code blue," the intercom shouted.

Mom took my hand and brushed the backs of her fingers along my cheek. "Oh no," she said as flashing lights swooshed across her shadowed face. She was wearing the same, faded heart-printed pajamas she'd been wearing every night in the ICU.

Medics ran an empty gurney past our room. "It's your friend, Matthew, down the hall," Mom said.

I had a friend here? Matthew's my friend?

"He went into cardiac arrest. He's the same age as you," she said.

Did we hang out? When did we meet? Did Drew know about this?

The next time I saw Drew, I forgot to ask if he knew Matthew.

Did any of them know Matthew?

When medics ran the gurney back down the hallway, there were yellow caution straps bound across a motionless, still-faced blonde boy.

Would I go into cardiac arrest too?

Mom kissed my forehead and slipped back into the cot beside my hospital bed. She pulled up her covers as the hum of my neighbors' ventilators and beeping heart monitors lingered. I closed my eyes. I didn't want to be here.

Although the lights had been off, somehow, the room felt darker than before.

Months later, Mom clarified that I never actually met Matthew. She said he was my friend simply because he was the only other young person on the unit, which sadly changed that night. Matthew didn't survive. May he rest in peace.

TWENTY-EIGHT

March 23, 2015

Pax's warm tenor rolled over my bedside. "Okay, Jen," he said, crinkling the long strip of plastic with the rubbery, red tube in it. "You know already, first we gotta suction and then we'll get you breathing on your own. Today is the twenty-four-hour trial."

Butterflies brushed the walls of my stomach.

It would be just me breathing; no help, no breaks.

Nurses' voices circled through my mind. The way they said, "Time for your medicine," each day while fully aware of the stupor they'd be sending me into, made me cringe inside. I had to get out of here and the twenty-four hour breathing trial was my only ticket out.

The light pressure of Pax's fingers on my trach triggered a pinching pain down the front of my throat. He unhooked the blue tube from the plastic spout in my neck and slipped the rubbery, red tube in. "Here we go with the suction," he said. The tubing whipped around as it did every day, scraping the insides of my throat. I couldn't breathe. My body flopped to the side, writhing in muscle spasms. My arms curled to my chest and legs bent up to my waist. My neck was rigid. My chin jutted forward.

I shouted inside, Jesus help me!

Globs of phlegm followed the red tube Pax slowly pulled from my throat. A deep cough erupted from my chest, triggering the continued thrashing of my body and relentless coughing that came whenever he manipulated my trach. My skin felt like it was burning. A stabbing pain consumed my muscles. My head rolled off my pillow, onto the mattress. My veins swelled along my hairline. I still couldn't catch a breath.

Jesus, help me!

Pax's gaze cradled my curled up, cramping body. A quick breath filled my lungs and shot out another roaring cough. My veins felt on the verge of bursting before another gasp of air filled my lungs. As my breathing began to outweigh my coughing, my shoulders relaxed back to the mattress. My legs sank together. My skin cooled.

Pax laid my head back on my pillow as he softly hushed, "Okay, okay." He attached my blue tube back to the plastic spout in my neck. "The ventilator is off so you can start breathing on your own," he said. "But you're still hooked up just in case."

He wadded up his latex gloves with the crunched-up wrappers, tossing them in the garbage as he neared the door. His band of braids turned as he looked back at me. He smiled and said, "You can do it Jen. I know you can."

Twenty-four hours was a long time to be breathing. But I breathed on my own before my injury ... no reason I couldn't do it again.

For the rest of the day I imagined the expanding and squeezing of my lungs as I chanted inside, In and out, in and out.

My stomach turned as Mom walked around my room in her burgundy-colored scrubs. It was her first day back to work. The sunrise was stretching through the half-turned blinds in the window, framing the oak tree outside. She walked back and forth from the bathroom to her suitcase, carrying her toothbrush, then her hair spray, then her makeup. She tilted her head, looking down the tip of her nose in the bathroom mirror as she glided a raspberry-colored stick across her parted lips. The diamond studs in her ears sparkled at the yellowing light fixture above the mirror. Short, blonde curls haloed her head. My trach blocked the sweet scent of her hairspray, which I used to smell every morning when I hugged her goodbye before she left for work.

"Okay baby," she said, slinging her purse over her shoulder. I used to call her purse her Mary Poppins bag because of its boxcar size and the bottomless pit it seemed to be; filled with cosmetics, wilted lottery tickets, travel-size deodorant, and popped sheets of Sudafed. "I gotta go to work now." She leaned over my bed rail, pressing her lips to my forehead.

My heart raced. I mouthed, No Mom, you can't!

The sheet of muscle splayed from my shoulder to my chin jerked the bottom of my jaw to the left. My lips formed a distorted oval shape. My top and bottom teeth slid in opposite directions. My left eye squinted as if to squeeze out a tear while the right side of my face lay flat. I sobbed inside, muted by the trach tube stretching from my throat.

"Honey, what's wrong?"

I mouthed, Please don't leave me.

Her green eyes turned glassy as she tilted her head. "Oh, it will be okay," she said and kissed the palm of my hand. "You'll have therapy this morning. Then, Tom is going to come and hang out with you this afternoon, and then I'll stop by after work, go home, and be back in the morning."

I mouthed, No! You can't leave!

My muscles continued to spasm, pulling my jaw in opposite directions.

What if I needed something? These nurses didn't know how to communicate with me.

Mom's lips parted. The creases between her brows deepened. "Okay, I'll stay tonight, I'll stay," she said, holding my hand to her chest. "I need to go to work though, honey. You will be fine today." She ran the palm of her hand over my forehead, brushing away my unruly strands of hair. "I love you," she said.

A woman in pink, flower-printed scrubs walked through the door. Rows of ebony-colored braids were perfectly lined across her scalp. She pumped the dispenser of sanitizer hanging on the wall and rubbed her hands together. "Hi ladies," she said with an overly animated smile. "My name is Kiki. I'm your nurse for today."

"Hi, I'm Jane," Mom said, shaking Kiki's hand.

They were making small talk when Mom nodded toward me, "She's a little nervous."

Kiki tilted her head, "Aw."

"Call me if there are any issues," Mom said. She leaned over my bed rail and pressed her lips to my cheek. "Okay honey, I gotta go," she said and slid out the cracked door. "Love you!"

My stomach dropped. I prayed, Jesus, please stay with me.

Kiki's smile flattened. She held up a syringe, pushing its tip into the opening of my IV and pumping a juicy, red liquid into the line draping from my arm. It was my morning dose of Oxycodone to relieve the pain that would radiate through my body when my muscle spasms kicked in. The liquid slid through the curves of the tube, slowly draining into the crease of my arm. Kiki kept her gaze down as she closed the cannula. She took the empty syringe, speckled with droplets of red liquid, and tossed it into the Sharps container mounted on the wall. She pulled off her latex gloves, threw them into the trash, and walked out the door.

My neighbors' ventilators hummed. The ticking of the red second-hand on the wall clock filled the gaps between the beeping of my heart monitor. My body lay still, bolstered by the pillows beneath it, as my mind began to sway. The clock on the wall magnified and shrank back to size, magnified and shrank back to size. The bulletin board melted into the wall as my hospital bed began to float.

I closed my eyes and sighed, surrendering to a dose of painkillers.

When I awoke hours later, Mom was still at work. It was just past noon and I was stuck within the tan, plastic rails outlining my hospital bed like a jail cell of sorts. My fingers pressed into the adaptive, silicone call light resting under my hand. I hadn't been strong enough to trigger the button but kept my fingers pushing. I was sitting in the swampy puddle of my own urine-soaked diaper, waiting for a nurse to serendipitously stop by. The wet cotton had faded in warmth, cooling along my bikini line up onto the small of my back. It was a pressure sore or an infection waiting to happen. The TV screen had been flashing its blinding light all day, playing soap operas back-to-back. I never could get into those shows.

A patient care technician lumbered through my door in cartoon, heart patterned scrubs. Her straw-colored highlights were grown out, starting an inch or two behind her greasy, brown roots. Thick strokes of eyeliner weighed on her drowsy eyelids, which curved down like the grimace pulling on her lips. Her voice was monotone. "What do you want?"

Geez.

My chest cinched. I wanted to shrink away or hide but had no choice.

I mouthed, I'm wet.

She turned to the cabinet behind her, pulling a new diaper off the shelf. She unlocked the bedrail, letting it slam down against the side of the bed. She stripped back my covers, piling the blankets onto my feet. She bent my right leg and folded it across the other. She crossed my arms over my ribs and rolled me onto my side. My right arm moved in slow motion as I reached for the opposite bedrail. My fingers wrapped around the plastic handle, hardly forming a grip.

She palmed my bony hip, tilting it forward as she pulled my soaked diaper through the backs of my legs. She lifted my leg as I waited for the cold wipe to smear between them. Instead, I felt the soft, dry fabric of a new diaper push back through my legs. Her hands tipped my hips back, putting me flat on the bed. She pulled the front of the diaper and flattened it over my abdomen. She unpeeled both sticky tabs and pressed them onto the diaper, pushing into my belly. She pulled down my hospital gown and pulled up on my covers, straightening them across my chest.

She didn't wipe me. She wasn't going to wipe me?

She stuffed a pillow under each of my arms and dropped the call light in my lap.

I still had urine drying on my legs. I wanted to tell her, I could get an infection!

She snapped the bedrail back in place. Her gloves slapped together as she stripped them off, tossing the stained wad of latex onto the pit of crumpled napkins and old styrofoam cups filling the garbage can. Then, she walked out the door.

I closed my eyes to pray, but my mind was blank. I hoped somehow God could find redeeming quality in a person like me who was giving even less to the world than that garbage can.

CHAPTER
TWENTY-NINE

March 24, 2015

MOM AND DREW stood in my room, talking as I basked in their presence. Both had the day off work. Russ, my speech therapist, stood with them as he sorted through his cart of therapeutic devices. He cocked his head, flipping the pesky swoop of his orange locks out of his eyes. The ends of his hair flared from the corner of his thick-framed glasses. He didn't look to be many years out of graduate school, but his calm demeanor and extensive knowledge made it seem that way.

My hospital bed groaned as Russ pressed the Up arrow on my call light, raising the back of my bed to a sitting position. My mostly limp arms and legs were held up with the usual number of pillows beneath them and the pin-rolled towel was wedged against the side of my head to keep it from flopping to my chest. My hair still had a close shave on the right half and whatever Mom or Drew were able to manage with a scrunchie and my long hair on the left. Mom and Drew stood at the foot of my bed watching Russ set up the electrical stimulation unit.

"Now, we'll put on the electrodes," Russ said as he peeled adhesive off of their dime-sized backs. "Are you doing okay?" With hands as gentle as his voice he stuck each electrode under the horse-shoe shape of my jaw-line.

I wanted to be mad at him, but he couldn't help how awful this treatment was.

I mouthed, Yes.

"Now the Coban," he said. He pulled on a corner of the roll of spongy medical tape, leading it around my neck three times. Its mesh fabric squeezed my throat, securing the electrodes onto my skin. The rash on my neck was spreading. The red spots were deepening under the humidity of the oxygen mask covering the plastic spout of my trach. I'd been breathing for more than 24 hours on my own, without the ventilator.

"Jen, I brought a slushy-type drink today," Russ said. He held up what looked like a yogurt cup.

Food?

My ears perked at the crinkling wrappers and tapping of plastic utensils on the particle-board end table beside my bed.

"It has a lemon flavor and honey-like consistency."

Yum, I liked lemon.

Russ lifted a spoonful of bright blue slush, taking me back to the Slushy machine waiting for every kid at the end of the check-out aisle in our lake town's grocery store. Above the row of tap handles was a puppy dog face printed on the front of the machine. He had a knit stocking cap and his tongue hung out the side of his smiling jowls, luring me in every time. When I pulled the tap handle, I watched the blue raspberry syrup slowly bleed through the mound of shaved ice in my cup. It was the same color of slushy Russ was preparing.

"Let's try a bite," he said, raising the spoon to my lips. I wanted to lunge at the blue, slushy liquid.

I opened my mouth to my first taste of food since February. Russ slid the white plastic spoon over my bottom lip and pressed down on the middle of my tongue. A gooey, bitter taste stung my betrayed tastebuds.

This wasn't lemon, lemon. This was Pine-Sol lemon, not Yoplait yogurt-dessert lemon.

Russ pushed his thumb on the red trigger wrapped in his other hand. The electrodes zapped my skin, making my tongue and neck muscles squeeze the bitter lemon down my throat.

"Good Jen," he said. He held out the empty spoon towards Drew, "Would you like to try feeding her and I'll stim?" Stim, meaning electrical stimulation or, in lay terms, the zapping electrodes.

"Sure," he said.

Drew took the cup and dipped the spoon into the slush. He held it up. "Ready?" He talked the way he always had, using the same tone of voice as the times he asked if I was ready to go for dinner or ready to run an errand. He knew under this strange, debilitated body was still Me.

He slid the spoon over my bottom lip, pressing its belly into my tongue as the cool, sticky liquid dripped down my chin. "Ah, shoot," he said, wiping a tissue across my face. "Sorry, that was my fault."

Would Drew always have to feed me? What would we do when we went out to eat?

Russ pushed the trigger. The electrodes buzzed and my throat squeezed another bitter teaspoon of slush down.

Drew dipped another spoonful and brought it to my parted lips

CHAPTER
THIRTY

March 25, 2015

GOOD MORNING AMERICA was flashing across the box TV hanging from my hospital room ceiling. Its lucid bands of light pinched my eyes. The back of my bed was raised to keep me in a sitting position. I had been breathing for more than forty-eight hours on my own and the oxygen mask over my trach kept my rash raw. I closed my eyes and tuned into the daily clamor of the nurses' station outside of my room. Blood pressure stands rattled as nurses wheeled them to and from their desk. Papers clapped against their Formica countertop as they shuffled documents into stacks. Clogs clip-clopped and tennis shoes squeaked over the glossy tile floor. I used to pass through those fast-paced nursing stations as an occupational therapy student. I would stop to type my notes in between-

My chest suddenly puffed out as I gasped. My head flew forward. Drops of mucus sprayed across my lap as I sneezed for the first time. My body flopped back against my mattress. The crown of my head bounced off my pillow and dropped to my chest. A burning pain trailed the back of my neck as my head dangled.

Oh, Jesus.

I could still see the nurses' station beneath my eyebrows. My right arm sprang from the mattress, swaying my limp hand back and forth. It leveled with my shoulder before plopping back down to the mattress. None of them noticed. I flung my hand in the air again, gaining half as much height as before.

I screamed inside, Jesus help me!

The burning pain hacked into the nape of my neck, like a knife scraping muscle off the bones throughout my shoulder. My voice was shrill as I prayed, Jesus, help me!

Body after body passed by my door without a glance.

Nurse. Nurse. Visitor. Nurse.

I waved my arm again. I was begging Jesus for help when my eyes locked with the woman whose power walking came to a dead stop. She stared over the shoulder of the gray sweater layering her scrubs. One of her feet stepped back, better aligning her gaze with mine. Her eyebrows scrunched and her chest stilled as if hesitating to ask a question.

I needed her help.

My hand jumped from the bed over and over.

She looked down, then turned back toward the hall.

I needed help. I needed somebody to help me!

My hand lay on the bed twitching, too tired to wave through the air. The burning pain in my neck stretched out to my shoulder. My screaming was muffling the activity at the nurses' station when another woman in patterned scrubs treaded down the hall. Her head was hanging low when she glanced toward my room. Then, she froze. Her one hand rested in the front pocket of her scrubs while the other cradled her clipboard.

I wanted to shout, Yes! I need your help.

Her eyes narrowed as she studied my collapsed body. She looked around, as if to see if other nurses were concerned. A hunchbacked lady was sorting papers at the nurse's station, another was leaning on a blood pressure machine as if gossiping with the other nurse typing on the computer beside her. The nurse before me switched the clipboard to her other arm and walked away.

No!

I sobbed and screamed inside. Jesus. Jesus, help!

It was as if each muscle fiber in my neck was shredding apart, as if the knife was digging deeper and deeper. The explosive chaos in my body was hushed by the normalcy of everyone else's day; beeping machines, trach tubes, paralyzed patients. It was nothing new.

Help me! Please, Jesus, please.

A pair of men's leather shoes screeched across the hallway tile. They didn't even come to a stop before their wooden soles ran toward me. His loose papers flew through the air. Two hands took either side of my face, lifting my eyes to his.

Dr. O'Malley.

His stethoscope lined the collar of his lab coat. Its round drum tapped the embroidery of his name. His papers were scattered across my lap and fanned out across the floor. He locked onto my eyes sitting between his hands. "Are you okay?"

My pain slipped from my neck like a cool sheet of silk, the moment he lifted my head. But my heart pounded.

Yes, I mouthed.

"Jenny," he said, catching his breath. "In your recovery you are going to have times of helplessness, but you have to be strong. You have to keep pushing." His voice sharpened, "You've got to promise me that you won't give up, that you won't lose hope, that you'll stay strong. Got it?"

Yes, I mouthed.

"Promise?"

His gaze seemed unbreakable from mine.

Yes. I promised.

CHAPTER
THIRTY-ONE

March 27, 2015

I WAS LYING in my hospital bed, waiting for therapy to start when the bold, black 27 printed on the wall calendar nagged at me. March twenty-seventh.

Why did it feel important?

My neighbors' beeping monitors and ventilators had become a sort of relaxing white-noise. The red second-hand on the clock above the calendar ticked to each dash mark around it. Its face must've been white or cream-colored back in its day but had since faded to a yellow-ish-beige like the floors.

Twenty more minutes until therapy. What would I do until then?

I wondered, as if I had a choice besides lying in my limp body.

My hand had been laid over the adaptive call light in my lap, shaped like a game show buzzer. My nurse said its soft, silicone top gave less resistance than a regular call light, making it possible for me to use. When we practiced, my fingers still weren't strong enough to activate the call. She said to keep trying throughout the day.

I pressed into its soft, gray belly, waiting for a voice to come through the intercom.

Nothing.

Oh, come on, I thought.

My fingers hyperextended as I pushed the button as hard as I could, but only silence filled the intercom. My eyes were cramping from the television light, which I couldn't seem to get away from. I closed my eyes.

I prayed, Jesus please be with me, please be with me, as I fell back to sleep.

My eyes bobbed open to the knocking on my door from Holly and Beth. "Hey, Jen! Ready for therapy?"

I always was.

I hoped they would stretch out the cramping muscles between my shoulder and neck. They'd been spasming, coiling themselves into knots since I arrived at the hospital.

Holly came to my bedside, asking, "Any pain today?"

I mouthed, Yes.

"Is your head in pain?"

No.

"Neck or shoulders?"

Yes!

"Okay, let me check out your shoulder, here." She felt around the side of my neck. "Your Traps are tighter than guitar strings," she said as she kneaded the cluster of knots, dissolving the pain. I hoped she'd never stop.

She asked, "is that feeling better?"

Yes, I mouthed.

When she pulled her hands away, my muscles squirmed for her touch. The knots recoiled into a pinching, cramping web of tight muscles.

"Alright, let's get you to the edge of the bed," she said as Beth removed the pillow propping up my feet. "How about getting those legs to the edge yourself?"

Like every other day, I tried to imagine the movement of my leg. In my wonder of how I slid my foot out before, I struggled to even know where my body was. Nothing but blank space filled my mind.

She pushed my left foot alongside the right. "Girl, we should get some music going, wake up these legs."

Music would've been nice.

The bold letters from the wall calendar stuck out at me, again.

Twenty-seven? I gasped, it was the day of the concert!

Drew surprised me with Mat Kearney tickets last month. We were driving in his car, heading into the city as lanes of concrete passed beneath us. Our hands were laced together over the console. The sweetness of his cologne was hypnotizing. I squeezed his hand and leaned closer each time I tried to guess what the surprise was. Never in that moment did I think I'd be spending my hours leading up to the concert in a hospital bed.

How would we get to the show?

My bed seemed to tighten its chains on my withering body.

Was he going without me? Drew would've needed to pick me up already if we were going to get into the city in time.

A pit dropped in my stomach. We were going to miss it.

But they, Mat Kearney, would still have the show. Other people could still go. No one else's life had stopped.

I imagined locks of long hair like mine, flipping over shoulders as friends and lovers lined outside the concert arena. Puffs of cold air would burst from their mouths as they laughed at a friend's joke. Their hearts would pound from a combination of excitement, alcohol, and trying to keep warm.

Beyond the concert, high heels still clicked over uneven sidewalks, briefcases swung beside fitted suits, paper bags crinkled in grocery shoppers' underarms, and drivers still sipped coffee as they sat in traffic on the expressway.

Life was still going on without me. People were still working, still shopping, still getting stuck in traffic. They were still going out, going to concerts. For nearly everyone else in the world, it was March twenty-seventh, another Friday night.

THIRTY-TWO

March 28, 2015

DREW WALKED THROUGH my hospital door in his black pea coat, hair combed to the side, button-down shirt and slacks. He smiled, making my insides turn to mush. "Hey," he said, coming to my bedside.

Two nurses followed behind him, pushing an empty gurney. One of them was the nurse with the greasy, grown-out highlights. The other I hadn't met. Her tall, thin frame pointed left to right as she told Drew they were going to get me out of bed. To sit in the "recliner," which was the spare gurney.

"We're going to change her first, so you can step out now."

Drew walked out to the hallway. The nurses flipped my body side to side, removing my wet diaper and replacing it with a new one. Praise God the tall one wiped me, cleaning off the urine I'd been sitting in.

They parked the gurney beside my bed and pulled the flat sheet beneath me, sliding my body onto the "recliner." Metal clanked as they raised the back rest. My head flopped down to my chest as they sat me up. My chin covered the spout of my trach, pinching my skin. A burning pain shot through the back of my neck.

"Are you comfortable?" The tall nurse asked.

I looked down, unable to open my mouth. I couldn't breathe!

"Okay good. We'll be back later to put you to bed."

No. I wasn't okay.

They walked towards the door as I screamed inside, Drew! Drew, help me!

He was still wearing his coat when he walked back into the room, hands in his pockets.

Drew! Please help me!

He squinted as he stopped in front of me. He tilted his head. "You're not comfortable, are you?"

I looked down.

He laid his hands over my temples and lifted my head back onto the pillow. The burning in my neck cooled. "I can't believe they left you like this," he said as he glared toward the door.

He looked up and down my thinning body, draped in a hospital gown and medical lines. He pressed the call light, asking the nurses to move me back to bed.

They came to my room, telling Drew it's good for me to be out of bed to build my endurance. But he insisted. They transferred me back to bed and later that evening, when they asked if I wanted to get out of bed again, I looked down and mouthed, No. Hell no.

CHAPTER
THIRTY-THREE

March 29, 2015

MOM WAS WATCHING me from the foot of my hospital bed as the pressure of Pax's fingers on my trach roused a clawing sensation on the front of my throat. He twisted a cap the size of a pencil eraser over the plastic spout stemming from my throat. The oxygen mask was gone. The cap would block air from moving through the spout.

I would have just my mouth and nose to breathe out of. It was how everyone breathed, but what if I needed more air?

There was a diagram of the lungs in one of my old textbooks. It showed an animated version of a pink ribbed trachea extending to each lung. Each one of those rib marks on the trachea now seemed more like little mile markers leading to the lungs. How would the air flow through my nose, down my throat, and into my lungs fast enough?

I shook off the thought.

I could do this. Just my mouth and nose. That was how I'd been breathing my whole life.

Pax's voice eased across my bedrail. "Jen, go ahead and try to say something."

My chest peaked as my mouth opened to say hi to Mom, but nothing came out. Pax pinched and wiggled the cap on my trach. It felt like pins and needles scratching the soft tissue of my throat, making my neck stiffen. My chin jutted forward as if to gag out the pain. The stiffness in my neck branched out to my shoulders.

The moment he let go, my pain ceased. "Alright, Jen. Try again," he said.

My chest swelled again as I dropped my jaw, letting noise pour from my mouth. "Hi," I said. My eyes widened. "I can talk!" My speech sounded primitive, more like I-an-awg! Each word tickled my sternum as air rushed through my trachea. I felt the way a baby must when she feels and hears her wild, untamed voice for the first time.

"Hah! Howhah! Haa," I shouted. My voice cutoff as my body suddenly fatigued.

Mom covered her mouth, hardly hiding the smile behind her hands. She let out a laugh of joy and relief, "Hi, honey!" She turned towards Pax to ask, "Why didn't I get that on video?" She dunked her hand into her purse, looking for her phone. "We have to call your dad!"

CHAPTER
THIRTY-FOUR

March 30, 2015

M OM'S WHISPERS NUDGED me awake. "Yes ... she felt sick ... they took her ...."

It was my last night at the vent-weaning hospital, and I was paired with the nurse I started with, Stella. Her soulful voice whispered back to Mom, "Oh Lord."

My eyes peered open. Mom was framed in the cut-out of my bedrail. She was sitting in her cot with her covers bunched across her lap. A ball of yellow light glowed from the lamp beside her as she looked up at Stella, who was standing with her hands on her wide-set hips. Her black and gold highlighted hair was braided and swirled into a bun, sitting atop her head.

She shook her head side to side as she hummed disappointedly, "Mmm-m-mm-mm-mm."

I shut my eyes so they wouldn't know I was awake.

They were talking about me! I bet Mom was telling her my story.

Her whispers came in mere puzzle pieces, giving a whole picture to Stella but only fragments to me, "She looked ... it was horrific ... she almost died."

What? I almost died?

Mom dished more puzzle fragments through the bedrail, "Her surgery ... didn't know," none of which I could make sense of.

Was it really true?

The thought was too complicated to dwell on. Imagining my own near death was like trying to grab the wind. I couldn't

When Stella left, Mom tucked under her blankets and switched off the lamp as I fell back to sleep.

CHAPTER
THIRTY-FIVE

March 31, 2015

A FTER MEDICS TRANSPORTED me from the vent-weaning hospital to my new rehabilitation hospital Mom and I spent the afternoon meeting my nurses and doctors and resting in my hospital room. That evening, Mom was sitting long-legged in the cot beside my new hospital bed. Her fingers punched the keys of her computer sitting atop the blankets in her lap. Its screen reflected in the lens of her glasses as we took on my first night as a city-girl. My new place was on the lakefront, outlined by streets I walked every morning and afternoon when I did my student rotation on the spinal cord unit here, last summer.

I got hooked on the rush only city streets give when Drew led me from the train station on our first date. Our hands bumped each other as we walked to the staccato of high heels clicking concrete and car horns yacking through the streets, electrifying my bloodstream. Late shift workers' office lights glowed out the windows of the buildings stretching into the night sky. Bands of city slickers brushed our shoulders, pushing us along the school of people with somewhere to be. I was trying to steady my clumsy breath when he said, "You can hold my hand ya know." His palm warmed mine as he laced his thick fingers through my petite ones, sending a burst of airy tingles swishing through my chest. Snowflakes cartwheeled from the sky, melting on my eyelashes. Crisp air slipped through my scarf to the back of my neck where his hands would hold to kiss me by the river on our second date. This kiss sparked the rapid growth of our relationship. In the weeks to follow we would confess our love for each other and start talking about what marriage might look like. I wanted to hold his hand as we walked through city streets and through life, forever.

I could feel those slabs of concrete racing under my feet from my hospital bed. My bed sheets wrapped me like the breeze made from taxis racing by. On the ambulance ride to my new hospital, we drove up Lake Shore Drive; a road Drew and I could never afford to live on. Yet, here I was, living on the lakefront.

Through the cut-out of my bedrail, I muttered, "Mom." My voice was slow, slurred and made 'Mom' sound more like, ah-um.

She kept her eyes and fingers on the computer. "Yes, honey?"

"Did I almost die?"

Mom's fingers froze. "What? Why do you ask that?"

"I heard you telling Stella."

"Well," she said, setting her computer aside. "Yes. You almost did." She looked away as if watching clips of that night reel through her mind. "You were really, really sick Jen. The first surgeon did not think you would survive, but there was another surgeon there who did. And he saved your life."

Her words were mesmerizing. How could something so drastic happen to me? And without me knowing? My life was average, not the kind that pushed to the extreme of death. I was near salivating for more details and asked, "What was it like?"

"Honey, I don't know if I want to talk about this right now." She tucked under her blanket a little further.

I was far too amazed by my own major life event, which I felt like I missed, to let the conversation go. "Does anyone know?"

"Yes."

"Do my cousins know?"

"Yes."

"Do my classmates know?"

"Yes."

"What was it like? What did you say to each other?"

"Honey, I really don't want to talk about it right now." She set the computer back on her lap, resting her fingers over the keys.

The sun had set, darkening my hospital room. The hallway lights glowed through the cracks of my door. Mom continued typing on her computer as I stared at the ceiling tiles. I was awestruck. How could that have happened? I had to know more, but didn't want to keep pushing. With no other option, I closed my eyes and fell asleep.

CHAPTER
THIRTY-SIX

April 1, 2015

UNBEKNOWNST TO US, inpatient rehab patients no longer wore hospital gowns. They wore their own clothes, but I had nothing besides the hospital gown I arrived in. Mom was still in her pajamas in the cot beside my bed when she made an early phone call to Drew, whose apartment wasn't far from the hospital. He dropped off his smallest pair of basketball shorts and t-shirt on his way to work.

The slippery black shorts were like a blanket over my thighs. My breasts hung freely in Drew's cotton tee. I wouldn't see the need to wear a bra until the night Drew and I discovered the length of my armpit hair. It was a couple weeks into treatment and about six weeks since they had seen a razor. Drew spotted my lengthening underarm hair while I was sitting in bed. He helped me reach, bending my arm and brushing my fingertips along the half-inch long hairs as my eyes widened.

What was I doing with my life? Letting my hygiene go like I was some sort of cave woman?

I demanded Drew call Mom, who had left for the night, to request she shave my armpits first thing in the morning. I started wearing a bra the next day and never looked back.

For the time being, I was free-breasting in Drew's clothes. Mom kicked off her tennis shoes. She was a half-size smaller than me but managed to squeeze them onto my feet. Mom pulled my hair into a ponytail. It was drastically thinner since my half head-shave from surgery. In the months to come, on the rare occasion I wore my hair down, Mom would comb it over to disguise the short hair. In that case, I looked like I had a regular head of hair rather than my signature poofed-out locks.

With my hair now pulled into a ponytail, I was officially ready for my first day of inpatient therapy. Mom said I had half an hour before physical therapy started. She swung her purse over her shoulder, said she was going to get a cup of coffee from the cafeteria, and stepped out the door. My room was quiet. The sunlight flowing in from the window made the grooves in the white bricks on my walls look creamy. In the coming days, the vanity sink facing my bed was the one I used as I brushed my hair on my own for the first time. The left side of my face beamed as I ran my wide tooth comb through my wet locks. I wasn't strong enough to reach the back of my head, but that would change in the days to follow.

For the present moment, I was lying in my new hospital bed, waiting for therapy, and excited by the feeling of clothes on my skin. A woman in dress pants and a floral cardigan walked into my room. The light moved up and down her glossy hair as she walked with a binder sitting against her hip like a baby. She asked for my name and date of birth to confirm I was, in fact, myself. She said she was my dietician and opened her binder, striking her pen against the pages of papers.

"It says here, you weigh 97 pounds. Is that right?"

My face scrunched as it could. I didn't think I weighed 97 pounds. That was what I used to weigh when I starved myself.

"I have you on a 2,000 calorie diet. Is that about what you usually eat?"

My eyes widened. Two thousand calories? I didn't eat nearly that much before. What numbers had I written in my food journal? One time I circled a total of 1,100 calories for the day, but that wouldn't be enough now.

The dietician waited with her pen point resting on her paper.

If only she knew who she was asking.

I wished Mom would walk through the door to decide for me. I needed my old notebook to see; in the dark green folder Sue gave me on our first appointment together. Where was my notebook? Two thousand calories was too much. I didn't want to get fat, but 1,100 wouldn't be enough.

"1,600?" I guessed. I wasn't really eating, anyway. I could only have tube feedings through the G-tube hanging from the left side of my abdomen. I hadn't tasted food since February, unless you count the lemon 'slushy' Roger fed me at the vent-weaning hospital.

The dietitian wrote down my answer without any skepticism, as if 1,600 calories would be enough to supply the energy I needed for recovery. She didn't know she was talking to someone who restricted her eating in an attempt to regain control of her life. Who was I to know how many calories I should be eating, anyway? She was the dietician.

"Okay, that's all I need. Let me know if you have any questions," she smiled and walked out the door. I didn't have any questions and that would be the last time I saw her.

Mom walked through the door, coffee in hand. She said the cafeteria didn't look as good as the one in Madison, but that would be okay.

A pair of physical therapists came into my room, stopping at the foot of my bed. "Hi Jen, my name is Lee. We're here to evaluate you for PT. Sound good?"

"Yeah," I said, which sounded more like, ah.

Like my therapy sessions at the last hospital, I attempted sliding my legs to the side of my bed and Lee helped to finish what I couldn't. He and his partner pulled me into a sitting position using the linen beneath me as a sling. I leaned on Lee as he pivoted me onto a tilt-in-space wheelchair. It had a headrest to bear the deadweight of my skull. It was like a stroller in the way someone had to push to get me around. Since I didn't have the strength to shift my weight, someone could recline the chair for me, taking the weight off my bottom and giving me what we called a "pressure break".

Lee wheeled me down the hall to the therapy gym where we would have our first session. Limestone arches and crown molding embellished the hundreds-year old buildings staggered in the floor to ceiling windows surrounding the gym. A strip of the lakeshore peeked out of the last window in the corner. Empty treadmills and mat tables lined the space between.

Sweet cologne drifted from Lee's neck as he sat on the doctor's stool in front of me. We were inside of the parallel bars as he wrapped a woven gait belt around my waist. Another guy in khakis and a polo shirt leaned against the parallel bars. "Hi Jen, my name is Nick. I'm your physical therapist." Lee was his student.

Nick held up a black colored sling and laced my limp, left arm through. Lee took hold of the belt on either side of my waist, saying he would help me stand up on the count of three. I leaned on his shoulder as his grip tightened. He gently rocked my body back and forth, pulling me to my feet on "three". A therapy aide grabbed both sides of my head to keep it above my shoulders.

I begged myself not to throw-up as the formula that flowed through my G-tube for breakfast that morning swished in my belly. It pinched the same way side-stitches used to on my long runs. My forehead suddenly felt damp. Blood felt like it was draining from my face.

Lee told me to step forward with my right foot. I curled my hand around the cool aluminum parallel bar beside me. My hips leaned into his shoulder as he hooked his arm around my backside. The sole of my foot slowly peeled off the ground. It felt heavy, as if I was stepping out of a mud pit. My knee marched in slow-motion, just high enough to clear my toes, before landing my foot back on the ground.

My first step.

"Good job, Jen! Now, kick out that left leg," he said. As my mind searched for the feeling of my left leg, trying to bend a seemingly non-existent extremity, he picked up my leg for me. "That's it! Kick, kick, kick!"

He told me to step right again. I slowly dragged my foot through the air and planted it back on the ground. He aligned my toes and suggested we take a break. "Lean toward me and stick your butt out," he said. He clutched the sides of my gait belt and sat me back into my wheelchair. The aide set my head in the headrest as blood re-surged to my face and my stomach suddenly settled.

Lee asked if I was up for walking to the end of the parallel bars, another five or six steps. "Then, we can call it a day," he said. The thought of more cramping and swishing liquid in my gut, more sweat beading across my forehead, more lifting of my lead-filled legs wasn't enticing, but I had to work to get better.

"Okay," I said.

That evening, Drew was sitting alongside my hospital bed, staring at the TV suspended from the ceiling. A vinyl curtain separated us from my roommate dying of a brain tumor. Her husband's loafer-clad feet occasionally paced along the bottom of the curtain.

Hospital blankets covered my worn, high school volleyball t-shirt from my one year on the B team. It was my last try at the sport before joining the dance team and eventually finding my niche in cross-country. After my first week of practice, I had bought two pairs of running shorts, one of which was hugging the diaper my nurse slid over my bottom earlier; a far cry from the lace thong I wore beneath my skinny jeans most Friday nights.

I should've been two blocks down from the hospital, where Drew and I walked the line of streetlamps that made snow-melting sidewalks glisten. Where car horns tangled with the static of bar-goers' voices shouting over the music beating on bar windows. My vodka-plumped vessels acted like little heaters strung through my limbs as Drew laced his fingers through mine; sort of how they were at the moment except resting on the edge of my hospital bed.

The cuff of his hoodie hid part of the plastic ID bracelet looped around my bony wrist. My fingers itched to walk up his arm and slip around the bulk of muscle shaping his bicep, where he'd pin my hand as I melted in the warmth of his body while we ran errands or burrowed in the couch for the night.

Suddenly, I wondered if he knew what Mom knew. I asked, "Drew, did you know I almost died?"

He scrunched his eyebrows. "Who told you that? I ... didn't think they were going to tell you."

"I overheard my mom telling the nurse at the vent-weaning hospital."

"Oh," he said, looking down. "Well, yeah. I knew."

"What was it like? Where were we? What did the room look like?"

"Jen, it was a nightmare. I'm sorry, but I don't really want to talk about it."

No one would tell me.

Reruns of reality TV flashed into his distant stare, a show about addictions. There was a woman who ate mattresses. She plopped chunks of foam into her mouth like popcorn. Her cheeks were round, squishing her eyes into half-moons. Her lips pulsed like a fish when she talked.

I gawked, "Drew, did you see that?" My voice was still hypernasal and slurred, sounding more like, Rew-id-you-see-ad?

I hoped the strangeness of my voice was just because of my trach, but soon I would have it removed and find my voice didn't change. Drew once told me how he loved the way I answered the phone, the way my smooth, feminine voice would say, Hi, how are you? made him swoon. I wasn't sure he'd get to hear my voice that way again.

Maybe he was uncertain, too. His face looked stone cold as a tear rolled down his cheek.

"Drew, what's wrong?"

"Nothing," he said, brushing away the tear.

My eyes widened, "Drew. What's wrong?"

"Nothing's wrong, Jen," he snapped.

"I saw a tear roll down your cheek!"

His lips tightened as he brushed his knuckle under another rolling tear. "I hate seeing you like this," he snapped again and turned back to the TV. He had a cold stare. One that was trying to keep everything about our current reality out.

His pain knocked the wind out of me. If I had claws to lunge at God with, I would've lunged. I prayed with blood-curdling rage, Why are You doing this? It makes no sense. I am hurting people just by being here.

My neck spasmed, jerking my lower lip into a half-frown and pulling my chin towards my shoulder. I fought the tears pushing on my eyelids.

Why would God do this?

CHAPTER
THIRTY-SEVEN

April 3, 2015

"PICK YOUR HEAD up, Kray," Nick said for the third time. He stood beside Lee who was at the front of my treadmill typing medical notes for his last day as a student here. "Get that left foot forward," he barked.

I groaned inside, It was going to be one or the other, Nick.

Either I could focus on keeping my head up or focus on moving my left leg, but I couldn't do both at the same time. It was too much to think about. My head was heavy. During other therapy sessions, my occupational therapist had me looking in the mirror while I lifted my head away from my wheelchair's headrest for one minute at a time. It took my full focus to do.

With Nick, I let my head lean on the wide straps extending from the sides of my harness to the ceiling. The harness was snug on my body. It kept me upright and caught me every time my left leg failed to step forward.

I was walking at .2 miles per hour. It had been twelve minutes and my skin was layered in a sheath of sweat. My morning tube feeding swished in my stomach, pinching the side of my abdomen.

"Kray, I heard you have a graduation coming up for OT," Nick said.

"Yeah, I do." May 8th was the day my classmates and I were to attend our hooding ceremony.

"What do you think about making your therapy goal to walk across the stage for graduation?"

"Yeah!"

"Alright, we'll do it. That'll be a good goal," he said, making a note on his computer. "And Kray,"

"Yeah?"

"Keep your head up."

CHAPTER
THIRTY-EIGHT

I WAS SITTING in my wheelchair, head leaning into the side of the headrest, at a table in the community room overlooking the lakeshore. My speech therapist put a light blue terry cloth bib around my neck that hung down to my lap. She uncovered the cafeteria tray sitting in front of me. A scoop of chocolate pudding filled the plastic crystal dish on the tray. I hadn't tasted food in over a month. My meals came through the tube hanging out of my abdomen. My nurse would hook up a bag of formula to the tube and let it flow at mealtimes.

In speech therapy, I had been practicing swallowing for weeks. At first I practiced by swallowing 50 to 100 times per session with only my saliva. After a week of that, I was approved to eat ice chips. One night I joined Mom, Dad, and Drew in the community room for dinner. They had deep dish pizza while I sat with my large styrofoam cup of ice chips. Per my therapist's request, I had to swallow twice before crunching on my next chip. I didn't even want the pizza. I'd had a much greater craving for inclusion, for having a spot at the dinner table. With my ice chips I officially did.

Nonetheless, chocolate pudding was an exciting step up. My therapist dipped the spoon, filling the tip with a glossy bite of pudding. I squealed as I opened my mouth. She pressed the metal spoon down on my tongue and slid it from my pursed lips, leaving a cool, sweet, velvety glob of pudding on my tastebuds.

My eyes widened. My left cheek pulled back in a smile as the sweet, cocoa flavor spread over my tongue before I swallowed. Then, I opened my chocolate-coated mouth for another bite.

For future sessions, I ordered whipped cream on my chocolate pudding. I relished the magic ice cream that came in a styrofoam cup. What made it magical was its protein content, its delicious chocolate flavor, and the fact it wouldn't melt. For patients with swallowing precautions like me, the magic ice cream was a god-send. In my six weeks at the rehabilitation hospital, I progressed to a full purée diet. I no longer needed the tube feedings as a supplement. I choked down puréed chicken when I had to and enjoyed cream of wheat in the mornings. Mom brought a small blender to purée black beans, rice, and salsa, which I liked.

I didn't think much about counting calories like I used to, probably because I couldn't. I had no resources to look up the calories of what I was eating, and I was too focused on re-learning to swallow in the first place. Any food I was strong enough to taste and swallow was a blessing.

The first time I was strong enough to receive Communion was at the Mass held in the basement of the hospital. Drew took me on Tuesday nights. I was only allowed a small piece of Communion because of my swallowing precautions—upon discharge, my therapist would say I progressed from severe dysphagia to bad dysphagia, which we celebrated. I didn't feel any radical change when I consumed Communion or anything, but rather a subtle thankfulness and sense of grounding. Either God was becoming more present to me, or I was becoming more present to Him.

CHAPTER
THIRTY-NINE

April 5, 2015

"ARE YOU READY?" My morning nurse was giddy as she parked me in my wheelchair, beside my bed.

"Yeah," I said as my stomach scooped an empty pit in itself. "Does it hurt?"

"I don't think so. None of my other patients have complained. He's good at what he does. He's taken out a lot of trach tubes."

I couldn't wait to sound like myself again, get this plastic thing out of my neck.

A short man, with a black, bushy mustache, carrying a briefcase knocked on the frame of my open door. He asked, "Jennifer Kray?"

My nurse rose to her tip toes and clasped her hands together, "Yes Carl! Come in, come in, come in!" She waved him on and leaned toward me. "These are my favorite days!"

Carl set his briefcase on my bed. He crouched before me, fiddling with the spout stemming from my neck. "It looks good. Ready to get your trach out?" His friendliness seemed overpromising on the pain-free front. But then, Pax came to mind. His long, banded cornrows. His hands, gentle yet able to send my body into a series of convulsive coughing by their touch. The pin-pricking feeling of the trach scraping my throat ....

"Yeah," I said, wanting to shrink into my chair.

Carl poked at my trach. "Okay, here we go! No need to be nervous here, Jennifer. I've done this plenty of times and before you know it, it will be out. In three, two, one." A short, white, plastic tube sat in his hand. "And there you have it," he said. "No more trach."

My nurse pulled her phone from her pocket and held it in front of our faces. "Want to see your stoma?"

"Yeah," I said, slapped by the hypernasal, slurred sound of my voice. Why did I still sound weird?

Our faces sat in the screen of her phone. My neck had a dime-sized hole that I hardly saw before she pulled her phone away. "Alright, now we gotta cover it up!" She said, grabbing a small square of gauze from the counter. She held it up to my stoma and placed a piece of medical tape along its sides. "There ya go," she said. "When you talk, press your finger over the gauze so air doesn't escape from your throat."

I pressed the gauze like an elevator button on my neck, saying, "Yep, thank you."

My voice still sounded martian-like. Why did it sound like that? Maybe once my stoma healed, it'd be back to normal.

"Hey, Jen!" My three cousins came through my hospital door, followed by my aunt and uncle. Mom and Dad pressed the call light, asking the nurse for help to get me out of bed. Cousin Bridget put a mason jar of wildflowers on my bedside table. "I thought these could brighten your room," she said.

It was Easter Sunday and nearly five weeks since Dad and I were out hunting. Other than my ambulance rides, I hadn't been outside since. But today was different. The nurse squeezed through my family-packed room. She raised the head of my bed so I was sitting, and swung my legs over the edge of the bed. She held my shoulders to keep me upright and leaned my body against hers. She held my waist and pivoted me into my wheelchair, where my head plopped against the headrest. Dad came behind my wheelchair as I said, "Let's go!" Which sounded more like, less-oh!

Down in the lobby, beyond the sliding doors was blue sky and sunshine. The smell of daffodils lingered from the last group of people busting out the sliding doors. There were two sets. One had to close for the other to open. As we waited in the space between them, the lull was enough to make me want to bust through the doors myself. When the second set of doors opened, the crisp lake breeze slid over my cheeks and neck. The fresh air flooded my lungs, replacing the shell of indoor air crusted around them. Sunshine soaked into my skin as I squealed.

The sun, it was the sun!

I closed my eyes, letting my body sink further into my chair. I stretched out my strong arm to take it in.

Blows of high-pitched noises rattled my ear drums as we headed toward the sidewalk.

What was it? I wondered as a dinged-up coupe rolled by.

A car horn. I hadn't heard one in over a month. Dad locked my wheelchair as he and the family sat along the curb beside me, a stone's throw from the bus stop I used to get to and from this hospital for my student rotation last summer.

Strangers passed by in business clothes. A man turned the corner on his bike, and another carried a coffee to-go. They were Real People. Each of them moved as if they had somewhere to be.

Were they going to work? To the store? To an appointment?

I'd never know. Ha! I didn't know them and they didn't know me. Those people had no idea what happened to me, who I was, or who I was with.

I sat in this same sense of awe when Mom and Drew took me to the grocery store for the first time. It was only one block east of the hospital, which made for an easy social outing. The store was dimly lit. The smell of rosemary and herbal supplements hung in the air. Shelves were packed with all kinds of canned and boxed goods. We crossed paths with even more Real People who would see me, but never know me. Likewise, I would see them, but never know them!

A woman in a trench coat glanced over as I picked out yogurt cups to bring back for speech therapy. What was the woman thinking? Did she figure I was a patient? Was she wondering why I was in a wheelchair?

Back on the sidewalk, Dad turned me around to face our family. They were sitting on the curb, standing around, unphased by the world's movements that so enamored me. The rays of sun gently sealed my eyelids shut, branching its warmth across my cheeks. Much like on my runs, I felt God's hands reaching through those rays, molding my heart the way He often did. My head leaned deeper into my headrest, letting the fresh air cleanse my mind.

That evening, Mom was in the bathroom getting ready for bed. I didn't need her to stay the night with me anymore, but she wanted to talk with the social worker who'd be stopping by in the morning.

I was laying in my hospital bed, under my usual set of extra blankets when my room suddenly began to dizzy, turning kaleidoscope shapes and colors. Triangles, circles, and squares overlapped each other. Blue, green, and red pigments melted together.

"Jen, speak to me," Mom said.

Where was she?

The turning of shapes and colors stopped, leaving me feeling like I was looking through orange-filtered glasses. I was standing in an empty, wood-paneled kitchen with plastic upholstered bar stools sitting under the overhang of its formica countertop.

"Jen, say something, please," Mom begged.

I couldn't. Where was she?

The scene of the kitchen peeled back like a page in a book, turning to a scene of a living room. Everything was now filtered green.

"Jenny," Mom raised her voice. "Talk to me."

I wanted to answer, but I couldn't speak.

Dana, my Polish nurse technician—who made me sleep in the buff one night to air out my skin. I didn't argue since she intimidated me—walked into the radically green-filtered living room. Velvety drapes framed the window behind the empty velour couch. There was shag carpet spanning the floors. Dana stood across the room in dark green scrubs, looking at me.

I asked, "What are you doing here?"

Before she could answer, a fluorescent light beamed out of the white brick wall, replacing the green living room. A wooden door appeared beside my vanity sink.

My vanity sink!

My hospital room patched itself back together, bringing me to the present moment of sweat streaming down my forehead. The hair behind my neck was soaked.

What was going on?

My body shivered violently as a group of nurses lined the perimeter of my bed. Mom leaned toward me, holding my hand. "Jennifer, you need to say something," she said.

My heart and breath were moving at speeds I hadn't felt before. Beads of sweat rolled down my face as I shook.

Why was it so hot?

Mom asked, "Can you hear me?"

The weight of my chest hardly allowed for the "Yes," I whispered.

The on-call doctor squeezed through the circle of nurses lining my bed. "The ambulance is on the way," she said. Mom looped clear tubing behind each of my ears letting the macaroni-shaped holes blow cool oxygen up my nostrils.

A pair of medics stormed my room. They transferred me to a gurney and rolled me to the elevators at the end of the hall. Mom hung onto my bedrail as we hurried through the deserted hospital lobby. Everyone but the guard at the security desk had gone home for the night. Cool, April air rushed across my face when the doors opened, leading to the ambulance outside.

I swayed side to side as they loaded me into the back. Mom held my hand and brushed my forehead as the heavy metal doors of the ambulance slammed shut. Moonlit buildings spun in the back doors' windows. The night sky was freckled with street lamps and store lights instead of stars.

On arrival I laid in the familiar quarters of an emergency room. Cold air. Fluorescent lights. The aroma of sanitizer. I was waiting to be taken to the CT scan. Nurses covered me with freshly warmed blankets. An IV bag hung from its tall, silver stand, reaching out to the crease of my arm.

This couldn't be happening again. Why would He bring me this far to have another brain bleed?

He wasn't.

Mom switched from lay woman to medical professional as she explained my symptoms to the emergency room doctor, prompting the young doc to give me valium, which knocked me out completely.

I awoke to Mom's voice as the fluorescent lights pried my eyes open. My body was still. My heart rate was back to normal. My skin was dry, no longer coated in sweat. Mom and the young doc were mumbling about seizure activity and Brainstem Release Phenomenon. We never would decide on a diagnosis besides, "Strange neurological reaction". Mom said she wanted to take me back to the rehab hospital, it was 3:00 a.m. Mom said I was looking better, more like myself. "I know my daughter," she told the doc.

Another doctor stepped through the doorway, confirming my CT scans were normal.

The bags under my eyes pulled down as I looked up to Mom. "I wanna go home," I said. Home as in Our hospital, where I'd been making progress and making memories.

The ambulance and transport medics took us Home soon after. The overnight security guard watched us roll back through the empty lobby at our hospital, which somehow felt less deserted than when we left. It was filled with peace. The gurney rattled onto the elevator, taking us to the ninth floor. Two lefts out of the elevator doors brought us back to my room on the right. For the days to follow, I feared the return of my symptoms as I went to bed each night. My sense of control over my recovery faded. I was motivated to get better, but this night reminded me my suffering wasn't necessarily over.

CHAPTER
FORTY

April 6, 2015

THE CORNER OF my lip pulled back toward my ear as my hospital bed, my sheets, my pillow held me in the morning light of my room. Mom rolled to her side, on the cot squeezed between my bed and the wall. She rested her head in her hand as she leaned on her pillow, whispering, "Are you awake?"

A woman in blue scrubs walked through my door. Her curly hair was tousled atop her head. She came to the foot of my bed, saying, "Well, I heard you had one hell of a night."

"She did," Mom said. "She's doing better though." She glanced at me, "Right, honey?"

"Yeah," I said. The dried ring of my eyelids burned from being up so late.

Pumping out hand sanitizer from the dispenser on the wall and rubbing her hands together, she said, "Well, my name is Amy." Her curls bounced as she talked, "I'll be your nurse today. You can rest a few more hours. Your therapy was moved back after last night."

I could've gone to therapy then if they needed me to. I had a never-ending supply of energy, it seemed. Maybe from all the weeks I was stuck in bed.

"Let's get you changed," she said, rummaging through the cabinets by my vanity sink. "You're wearing pull-ups, right?"

"No," I said, although I wished I was. I'd been wearing bulky diapers since I left the ICU more than five weeks ago. I was offended when one of my nurses mentioned my incontinence to another. I knew when I had to go to the bathroom. I just couldn't hold it.

The plastic bikini lining of the diapers my nurses had been putting me in, cut across the tops of my thighs and were taped together higher than my belly button. Pull-ups seemed more discreet, more like real underwear.

"What? No one has gotten you in pull-ups yet? You haven't had an accident in three or four days, right?"

"No," I said.

"Well, today's the day. You don't need diapers anymore," she shrugged and waved her hand at the thought.

My eyes lit up.

Was she serious?

As she tore open a new package of pull-ups she mumbled, "Yeah girl, you're totally ready for this." She came to my bedside, stripped me of my diaper, slipped the pull-up up my legs, and gave me back a small piece of my dignity.

Wearing pull-ups was drastically more comfortable. They didn't have the bulky material diapers had which created a bulge in the front of my pants. Drew was the first to point it out.

A couple days after meeting Amy and staying dry in my new undergarments, I was sitting in my wheelchair, beside my bed, watching TV. I was watching one of the many wedding-themed reality shows. I enjoyed judging the new brides as they picked out their wedding dresses for thousands of unnecessary dollars.

I had an hour to burn before my next therapy session. The dog-shaped chia pet sitting in my windowsill had already been watered and turned for the day. I was anxious to trim the green sprouts bushing out from its sides. In addition, I already had my lunchtime tube feeding so there wasn't much to do but watch brides dress shop on TV. It was during the final dress try-on when a dull pressure pushed on my bladder. I had to pee.

My bathroom needs were urgent. The muscle strength I needed to hold it hadn't recovered yet. I also wasn't strong enough to transfer to and from the toilet on my own. A nurse had to bear-hug me to get me from my wheelchair, onto the toilet. My core was too weak to keep me sitting up straight, let alone standing. My knees were notorious for buckling and my center of gravity was off.

I pressed the nurse button on my call light and tried rocking side to side, though my body wasn't moving much. My call light was on. Maybe someone, anyone would instantaneously show up. Several minutes passed and the pressure on my bladder pushed harder.

Suddenly, a warm liquid trickled out of me. It wet the insides of my legs, making my running shorts stick to my skin. It seeped into my seat cushion, gushing beyond the boundaries of my pull-up.

Then, the nurse technician walked in to ask what I needed. Her name was Keesha. Her cheeks were round like her belly, and she breathed heavily. The first time we met I had diarrhea bubbling like lava down my legs after a dose of Miralax and Colace kicked in. To the doctors who order laxatives and stool softeners for their patients who only consume liquified food through their G-tubes anyway, I ask, Why?

Keesha's puffy lips separated and her eyes half-rolled back when I confessed, "I had an accident."

She transferred me back to bed, leaving me in my wet shorts until she was ready to change me. She peeled off the velcro seat cushion from my wheelchair. Her eyes were narrow as she slipped off its cover to clean it. "You shouldn't be in pull-ups if you're going to have accidents," she snapped. "If you have another one, I'll put you back in diapers."

I wanted to curl up in the corner of the room like a dog with its tail between its legs. Had she gotten to my room sooner, we wouldn't have had this problem. Yet there she was, glaring as she wiped down my wheelchair and betting I'd have another accident.

I didn't.

FORTY-ONE

April 12, 2015

MY MUSCLES SQUIRMED, stretching in different directions across my hospital bed, which had a lake-view. After hearing mention of rooms with a lake view, Mom had the nurses move me from my original room with no view, to this one. It was one of the prized hospital rooms and the best residence I'd have as a city girl. While I was usually looking out at blue water, at the moment it was dark. Framed in my window was the midnight sky that turned the sleepy lake waves into rolling black ink.

The blue portable vitals machine I saw every six hours stood beside the technician peeling back my bedsheets. Her eyes widened at the sight of my abdomen. She covered her mouth. "Oh, no," she said. "I'll be right back."

What?

My head was glued to my pillow, still too heavy to lift. I could see only the bunch of white linen.

What was that about?

My nurse power walked through the door to my bedside. "I'm gonna take a look at what's going on here," she whispered. She pulled back my bunched-up bedsheets and gasped. Her hand plunged into her pocket, pulling out her clunky work phone, which looked more like a walkie-talkie. She raised the head of my bed, bettering my view.

The bottom of my white t-shirt was rolled up under my bra, avoiding the blood smeared across my abdomen. A tangle of plastic tubing was sitting beside me.

What was that?

My nurse pinned the phone between her shoulder and ear, talking with the on-call doctor. "Okay, yeah ...," she said, stripping apart a long, narrow casing. She pulled out what looked like a jumbo drinking straw.

"Stick the catheter in," the gravelly voice mumbled from the other end of the phone, "To keep it from closing."

Slowly, she pushed the catheter into the wet, red hole in my belly. A dull poke pressed on the back of my stomach when the phone mumbled, "Be careful because if you go too far, you'll puncture the stomach."

The poking stopped. She held the remaining catheter like a stirring spoon sticking out of my gut. "Yep, it's in," she said. "Yeah, the tech is right now ... okay ... I'll ... oh wait, she's here."

The technician returned with a fresh loop of tubing in hand. My nurse re-pinned her work phone to her shoulder, taking hold of the new tubing. The hollow plastic cylinders traded spots, sliding in and out of my stomach like engine oil dipsticks. She wiped the blood from my abdomen. The technician helped change my stained sheets, rolling my body side to side while spreading a fresh draw sheet beneath me. My nurse unrolled my shirt to meet the waist of my running shorts. She stuffed a pillow under each of my arms and pulled my blankets to my chest. She clicked off the lights and left, letting the view of the ink-filled lake rock me back to sleep.

FORTY-TWO

April 16, 2015

"HERE IT IS, Kray," Nick said, leaning against an empty wheelchair with a smirk across his face. Drew was behind me, still wearing his coat since getting here from work. He wheeled me closer. The hall had quieted since the afternoon had passed. The tile floor was like a runway beneath us, waiting for a new set of wheels to coat its path.

That was for me?

Its matted, navy-colored frame ran under the black seat cushion. Shiny, orange cylinders swooped and dipped into footrests.

Chicago Bears colors. That was sleek.

Tires as big as bicycle wheels sandwiched the chair's sides. A ring of aluminum lined the spokes' edges, where I could push to propel the chair on my own. The mesh back was only tall enough to touch my shoulder blades. No headrest.

"If you want to go out for lunch with rec therapy on Monday, you gotta use a manual wheelchair," he said, patting the handlebars.

A manual wheelchair. No headrest. What if I got too tired of holding my head up? What would I do? There was no tilting feature, what if I needed a pressure break?

But it looked so cool.

"Come on Kray, let's do it," Nick said, squaring the chair up with mine. He held my waist as I clutched his shoulder, rocking me three times before pulling me to my feet. My feet followed his, sidestepping in front of the new chair. I bent forward as he said to push my butt all the way back in the seat as a cushion scooped under my thighs. Spongy, mesh backing followed the slight curve of my rib cage like the driver's seat in my car.

Nick tightened the seatbelt across my waist. "Alright, it's all you," he said and reached over to unlock the brakes of the old, empty wheelchair. He grabbed its handlebar and power walked behind it. "See you Monday," he shouted back, shrinking as he walked further down the hall.

Drew slipped his phone out of his pocket, pointing its camera lens at me. He nodded, cueing me to roll the new wheelchair on my own. The smooth aluminum ring lining the tire cooled my hand. I pushed and released, letting the aluminum brush through my fingers until it slowed. I gripped it again and pushed. The rubber toe of my tennis shoe tapped the tile floor, steering the chair left or right. The slick, tile squares beneath me were like an ice rink gliding under my wheels as I bumped into the wall, scraping along scuff marks other wheelchairs had hit many times before. My head tilted as if to feel for the curve of my long-gone headrest.

It was all me.

CHAPTER
FORTY-THREE

April 24, 2015

S WEAT WAS SWIMMING between my palms, clasped in my lap. Thin, blonde hairs arched out of the puckered follicles dotting my arms. The doctor stuffed his hands into a pair of latex gloves, snapping them against his wrist. The cursive embroidery on the front of his white coat read, Dr. Brutta. My speech therapist sent me to him. She said he had a treatment that could help fix the slur in my speech. The procedure chair was like a pedestal perching me just above his 5'9" frame. Mom set down the copy of *Family Circle* she pulled from the magazine holder before he walked through the door.

Why did I have to do this? Really, I thought, I'd be okay without it.

"So, this will be uncomfortable," the doctor said, "but I promise to make it as painless as possible." He tilted his head and smirked.

I didn't want to do this. Why couldn't we just let everything come back naturally?

He set his hands on his hips as if to dare me. "Say Coca-Cola for me."

My C's melted into G's. "Goga-Gola," I said.

"See," he turned to Mom who inched closer to watch the procedure. "If we inject the small palate with gel to plump it up, we can get her to pronounce those K sounds better."

Cabinet doors clapped open and shut as he collected supplies. Plastic wrappers crinkled and buttons clicked when he turned around with a four-inch-long needle attached to the goop-filled syringe in his hand. "Go ahead and open," he said.

He centered the needle in the open space of my dropped jaw, like a hunter drawing his bow and arrow. Squeezing my eyes shut, I could still sense the needle's body hovering in my mouth. Its tip stung as it sank into the plush tissue ending the roof of my mouth for one, two, three seconds.

He pulled back the needle. "Say Coca-Cola for me."

"Goga-Gola," I said.

He scrunched his face at Mom. "She definitely needs more."

No! I was sure I'd be fine.

"Open again for me," he said, holding the syringe off to the side like Marilyn Monroe's cigarette.

My jaw dropped slowly. The needle sank back into the soft tissue on the roof of my mouth. My hairline dampened with sweat for one, two, three, four—

Dr. Brutta hopped backward with the needle in hand. "Say the word, Jen!"

"Goga-Gola."

He whipped his head toward Mom, then back at me. "We're gonna try this one more time," he said.

What? No.

Mom was standing with her arms crossed, waiting for him to continue the procedure.

Did she not feel the heat of the stare I was giving her to intervene? I didn't care what I sounded like. I didn't want to do this anymore. Although, my speech therapist said the patients who braved this procedure before had improved because of it. Plus, Nick and the rest of my team all knew I was seeing Dr. Brutta. They were all expecting me to progress from this treatment. I had to do it.

For a third time, my jaw dropped open as Dr. Brutta held the needle before my mouth.

I groaned inside, Just get it over with.

"Here we go," he said. The needle pinched, pushing deeper, towards my throat for one, two, three, four, five—my face scrunched. The crown of my head pushed into the headrest as my shoulder blades dug into the back of the chair. The needle sank deeper. A sharp pain branched across the back of my neck like cracking ice, shooting to my head and shoulders.

I shouted inside, Stop! Stop!

My hand raised to shove his hand away. The hair on his arms brushed my fingertips as he jumped back with the needle. Tears welled in my eyes as my neck stiffened. When I tilted my head toward Mom the same sharp pain shot up my neck.

Something was wrong.

My forehead and underarms broke into a sweat.

He hopped onto his back foot and pointed at me. "Say Coca-Cola for me!"

"Gogka," pain shot through my neck on each syllable, "Gkola".

"There we go, I'm hearing that K sound now," he told Mom. "Some people continue to see results a few days or so after the injection."

I spoke quietly to lessen the zing in my neck as I asked, "Is it normal to feel pain?"

"Yeah, you might feel a little sore for a day," he said.

Mom watched the words slither off his lips. I stared at her again, hoping she'd feel the pressure of my gaze.

I wasn't just sore.

Mom and I returned from our one-block walk from Dr. Brutta's office back to our hospital. Every crack and bump in the sidewalk that ran under my wheelchair sent the zinging pain through my neck.

Now, I was sitting in the least painful position with my chin turned slightly to the right, toward the view of the lakeshore in my hospital room window. Tears bubbled along my eyelids.

Dad was sitting on the edge of my bed. He asked, "Honey, what's wrong?"

"My neck is killing me. I can't move without making it worse."

Mom hurried through the door, announcing, "I got you an extra hour of PT with Meg! She'll be ready in fifteen minutes."

"I don't think I can," I whispered.

"You have to. Meg is nice enough to give us the extra therapy time." Mom said.

"I can't," I said. My bubbled tears began rolling down my cheeks.

"You're probably just having a muscle spasm."

"It's not a muscle spasm. It's from that shot."

Dad interrupted, "Why don't we ask the nurse?"

My afternoon nurse paged the doctor who ordered me a double dose of Motrin. Mom stomped into the hallway where Meg was waiting. "She's actually not coming to PT," Mom said.

The nurse raised the hem of my old running shirt above my belly button, thumbing-open the plug at the end of my G-tube. From the syringe in her hand, a double dose of Motrin sloshed through the tube, swirling into my stomach. She lifted a cup of water, tipping its edge to the opening of the plug. As the water flowed through the tube, a cool sensation breezed through my sternum, around my lungs, and back to my belly. She recapped the plug and tucked the tube back under my running shirt, which I earned from the half-marathon I ran the year before. That spring day had been sunny and cool, not as warm as the fresh air now sitting outside my hospital window.

The sun beamed through the glass, warming my skin. Nine stories down, people crawled across their yachts like ants, anchored along the lakeshore. Mellow waves rolled under their boats' bellies, hardly making them move.

My neck suddenly loosened. The pain that sprawled my head, neck, and shoulders melted away.

"Dad," I said. "Let's go down to the gym. I wanna walk."

CHAPTER
FORTY-FOUR

May 3, 2015

I WAS SITTING in my wheelchair with Mom at my side as the boats along the lakefront filled my hospital room window. If only it could open to let the crisp, cool lake breeze brush over my skin. It would balance the sun beaming through the glass, warming my bony legs.

Mom rolled my bedside table closer, resting her feet on the metal frame connecting the wheels. She put her computer next to the container of purple putty I'd been using to strengthen my hand. I was supposed to squeeze the putty, roll it into a snake, and poke my fingers into it; something I learned about in school.

Mom opened her computer and looked at me, asking, "When do you want to take over the blog?" She started a blog when I was in the ICU to keep family and friends updated on my progress. People were asking when I would start writing.

"I was thinking once I'm discharged. But I thought it'd be cool if I wrote a post before then, like a sneak peek."

"Good idea. You want to try writing a post right now?"

"I don't know what to write," I smiled, bashful at the thought. "What should I say?"

She scooted her computer toward me, "Just write about your day, how you're feeling, what you've done."

The light of the computer screen pushed a dull pain through my pupils. My vision jerked the keyboard side to side, up and down from the constantly jumping world my nystagmus had me living in. One morning in occupational therapy I was shaken by something else different about my eyes.

My therapist was standing behind my wheelchair, watching me wash my face at the bathroom sink. My fingers stopped the soapy cloth at the top of my cheekbone when I caught sight of the direction of my eyes, asking, "Am I cross-eyed?"

"No," she said. "Your right eye is deviated inward, so when you turn your head to the left, it looks like your eyes are crossed." My right eye was fixed inward, looking toward my nose, but my left eye moved freely. I kept my gaze forward and turned my head to the left, watching my eyes cross. I looked forward again and turned my head to the right until my eyes aligned. Turning my head to the right made it easier to see the keyboard.

Mom's acrylic nail tapped the Journal app on the screen for me. She'd had a French manicure on her nails for as long as I could remember, which, by default, is how I liked mine painted, too.

A blank page filled the screen. My right hand grazed the keyboard, seeing if any of the keys would guide my fingers for me. Mom pulled out a magazine and leaned back in her chair. None of the keys stuck, so I started with my day:

It was a frustrating morning. The tone in my leg was so bad, it was the worst I had done on the treadmill by far. However, I know I need to stay positive. I'm starting to take my pills by mouth, crushed in applesauce. I was able to do sit ups for the first time yesterday, which was very exciting for me. It is starting to get warmer outside. We went to Navy Pier yesterday and I had so much fun with Mom, Dad, and Drew. We had perfect weather to walk around and take some pictures. While I have very little control over my tone, I have complete control of my attitude. I knew eventually I would have a bad day on the treadmill, just like the days I had bad runs. But trying always feels better than nothing. No matter how fast I'm going on the treadmill or in the hallway, it always feels like a run which I would only dream about before my stay here.

Many of my dreams are coming true. I feel so blessed every day. I have my low points at times. However, at the end of the day I always feel like my normal self and am grateful for that. I am still successful, smart, hard-working, and most importantly faithful. Though I may not understand everything right now, I don't need to. God's plan will always prevail and will be better than I could have ever imagined. I am so lucky to be experiencing this. My journey has made me a much stronger individual. I feel beautiful and thankful every day. I have supportive and loving family and friends, and I was able to enjoy much of my time with them today. Additionally, I have Drew; a strong, intelligent, loyal man who refuses to ever give up and truly has helped me to create a solid foundation in order to be successful in rehab.

Thank you so much for your love and support during this journey.

Looking back on this post, today, I can confirm these feelings were true. I really did feel blessed. I wasn't constantly jovial, wheeling my way through the hospital and throwing confetti at the nurses in celebration of all the suffering I endured. I was positive, optimistic, and motivated to recover. I had an instinctual sense to trust there was something bigger than myself, bigger than my circumstances, at work. The most important parts of my life seemed to be under one roof, my roof, at the hospital.

Every day, I was surrounded by people my age, who also had degrees in therapy, cheering me on as I got stronger. My life was suddenly flooded with new experiences. From my first time talking to my first time eating, my first time brushing my hair, my first time at a grocery store to my first time receiving Communion. Mom and Drew would take me to one of the other hospital floors for K9 therapy and art therapy every week.

My support system was nationwide. Friends and family from California to North Carolina and many states in between sent packages, cards, commented on Mom's blog, visited, and prayed for me. What filled my heart the most was my time with Drew. When we weren't at one of my therapy sessions, we used the dry-erase side of Charlie's Board to play Hangman. He stumped me once, under the Food & Drink category, with the word Guava. Another evening, I was in my wheelchair while he sat on a doctor's stool, twirling me around the community room as we danced to the beat of our own laughter, on our own wheels.

One of the days Drew was gone, Mom and Dad were sitting on my hospital bed when they told me I should check my phone. I hadn't seen it since the morning of my brain bleed and I didn't want to see it now. That little, black rectangle felt like a tracking device; anyone could reach me anywhere, anytime. But Mom and Dad insisted. I took the phone from Mom's hand. Its screen light was hard on my eyes, but on it were messages from Drew. A message from the day after my surgery. A message from the first day I moved my arm: *Hey babe. I'm sitting at your bedside, holding your hand. You moved your arm for the first time today. I'm so proud of you. I love you.*

Tears blurred my vision. Mucus streamed from my nose as I began to sob.

"Keep reading," Mom and Dad said. I wiped my sleeve under my nose and held out my phone for them to read his messages to me.

Why did Drew love me? I didn't deserve him. He didn't have to live this way, with the burden of my disability. I did. He could go on and have a good, easier life. He didn't have to stay with me.

But he did. I was blessed.

CHAPTER
FORTY-FIVE

May 8, 2015

THE HEAT FROM a curling iron rose along the back of my neck. A freshly curled ringlet of hair dropped to my back.

"Almost done," my occupational therapist said.

Mom was at the foot of my wheelchair, trying to shove one of my Keds shoes over my braced foot. The AFO, ankle foot orthotic, was a bulky brace but kept my foot from flopping down when I walked.

"Close your eyes," Rachel said. A burst of sticky, fruity-smelling spray clouded my hair. She wheeled me to my bathroom sink. "Take a look," she said.

Long, brunette waves framed my face. They were combed over to cover the buzzed half of my head. My eyelashes fanned out from my blue, asymmetrical eyes. My partially paralyzed lips were painted a cinnamon-pink.

Mom walked up behind me. "Come on, honey, we gotta go," she said.

It was a three-hour car ride to my alma mater, and, per doctor's orders, I had to be back by midnight.

Drew and Dad stood at my hospital room door in their suits, with a bouquet of flowers. Mom followed as they wheeled me to the downstairs lobby, leaving Rachel and the rest of my rehab world behind.

My shoulders barreled into Drew's lap as Dad drove along the curve of lower Wacker Drive. We were graduation-bound, but going to make a pit-stop in the suburbs, at home, for a driving break.

Our leather-bound backseat was slick under the skirt of my dress. What used to feel like a slight right now felt like a sharp right. Our tires were spinning in a high-pitched hum as we sped through a dimly lit tunnel. Headlights from the other side of the road rushed toward us, swelling across our windshield until they cut to the side last minute, staying on their side of the road. It felt like a game of Chicken.

Drew cupped my shoulders, pushing me upright as our car slowed before a red light. Dad loosened his grip on the steering wheel. Mom poked at her phone while Drew stared out the window, occasionally checking on me with a head nod and a smile as we drove my old work route back home.

How did they know the other cars would stay on their side?

An hour into our drive, wide, green leaves filled out the Maple trees lining the side of the road and our town. My friends' houses scrolled across my car door window. Most were two-story homes, faced with brick, and with an SUV in the driveway. The running path Molly and I spent miles and miles on, ran alongside our car tires. Dad turned past the red flashing light hanging in the intersection and veered into our driveway. Helicopter leaves covered the blacktop, wet after the early morning rain.

I was home!

Light blue wood sided our house the same way it had since we moved there on my first birthday. Dad taught me how to hop our wooden fence when I shot the basketball into our backyard during a game of HORSE. Our basketball hoop stood tall in the cement he poured when Tom and I were still too small to use a regular basketball.

Dad pressed the rectangular button clipped to the sun visor. The garage door grumbled as it rolled open and he parked in front of it. Seatbelts and car doors unlatched, letting the dewy air moisten my skin. He helped me out of the car, pulling my legs around the side of the seat, hugging my waist, and sliding me out of our SUV. My palm pressed to his, using his hand as a substitute for my cane. I swung my left leg out to the side and forward to step ahead, walking the same path I took to start and end my morning runs.

The shade from the garage cooled my skin. The smell of metal and sawdust drifted from the pegboard decorated with tools Dad seemed to always find use for. The rusty nuts and bolts cabinet has been planted on the edge of Dad's work bench for as long as I remember. A series of pen marks lined the wall along the door leading inside. Each dash of ink was made by Dad who measured my and Tom's height every birthday. The boom-box I used to sing and dance to as a kid, sat beside Molly's forty-pound bin of dog food. Her chicken flavored kibble was the last whiff I got before Mom opened the door for us. She didn't seem to notice the knob's faded gold paint in the keyhole or the splotch where twenty-two years' worth of palms had touched.

Where was Molly?

Her paws tapped the hardwood outside the laundry room, but she wasn't coming. As we turned into the living room, there was our brick fireplace, the one I used to perform my concerts on. The grandfather clock was still standing in the corner next to the antique butter-churn, which we used as a side table for the lamp.

Then, there was Molly! Our neighbor sat on the couch, keeping a short grip on Molly's leash. Dad sat me on the loveseat, where Molly and I used to snuggle. Mom and the neighbor's voices overlapped as they told Molly, "Settle down!"

"Let her go," I said. I hadn't seen her since the morning we went hunting, the morning she watched medics load my half limp body onto a gurney and hurry out the door. I wanted her to jump on me with her usual attack of kisses.

Our neighbor let up some slack on her leash. Molly lowered her head as she inched toward my legs with a caution I didn't know she had. She sniffed my shin, then the hard plastic AFO covering my other leg. I rubbed my thumb along her velvety ears. She backed her head away, shifting her amber eyes over my slumped body on the couch. She knew it was me.

"Okay honey," Mom said. "You need to go to the bathroom 'cause we gotta hit the road. We don't want to be late for graduation."

The remaining two-hour car ride brought me to the blue and white tassel hanging from my graduation cap. Its silky strands swayed every time I moved my head. My black, polyester gown fit me like a pillowcase, draping over the sides of my wheelchair. Dad, Drew, and I waited in line with my capped and gowned classmates between the tall, dark, velvety curtains hanging from my college's theater ceiling. Graduate students and family members filled every one of the auditorium seats.

Katie, who gave me my first laugh in the ICU, walked into the glow of the stage lights. She stopped at center stage, standing before the audience as the light blue hood was placed over her. She shook the hands of our professors lined up on stage. My next classmate walked out into the beaming spotlight at the sound of her name on the auditorium speakers.

I was next. Dad and Drew hooked their arms under mine and hoisted me out of my wheelchair. Dad held my spastic, left arm that straightened itself anytime I exerted myself. Drew took my right hand as he would to put a promise ring on my finger that summer.

Dad looked over at me. "Ready?"

I nodded. We stepped out of the shield of curtains. The slow clack of Dad's and Drew's dress shoes seemed amplified by the silent, waiting crowd. As we neared the spotlight, I recited my new mantra, Don't cry, don't cry, don't cry.

Lynn, who was our instructor the day Hal's penis fell off, watched me from the podium. She leaned toward the microphone. "Jennifer Christine Kray," she said.

Tears burst from the corner of my squinting eye, the eye that moved. My lip pulled down as the left side of my face scrunched. My jaw craned toward my shoulder. My arm and leg stiffened. The right side of my face lay flat, lifeless. My tears gushed and my jaw cranked further at the feeling of its stillness.

Jon, who I hadn't seen since the ICU, was waiting in the buttery-colored spotlight sprawling across center stage. The last time he saw me was in the ICU with a bandaged head and ventilator tube; when I was only able to move my eyes and the tip of my right thumb.

Dad and Drew stopped me in the wide circle of light, turning my back to Jon and facing the audience. My cheeks warmed in the light as Jon lowered a blue sash over my head, draping it across my neck and shoulders. My hood.

My body careened toward Dad then Drew, waddling as I turned around to face Jon. My one arm hooked around Jon's neck as I sobbed in his ear. The remainder of my professors stood shoulder to shoulder on stage, clapping as I hooked my arm around each one of them for a hug.

My wheelchair had been moved and was waiting for me at the edge of the curtain leading offstage. My head hung as I cried and Dad and Drew backed me into its seat. I collapsed into the cushion, wiping tears from my cheek. Dad shouted in my ear, "Jen, look at the audience!"

Every person was on their feet, clapping and whistling. I let out another sob and waved.

In the year to follow, I had to give up my dream of becoming an occupational therapist. I wasn't able to meet the physical requirements necessary to finish my fieldwork. If I couldn't work in occupational therapy, I wanted to do something with Faith, but what?

CHAPTER
FORTY-SIX

May 18, 2015

MOM, DAD, AND I got back to the hospital at 11:20 p.m., making my midnight curfew. After ten more days of walking on treadmills, practicing swallowing, and improving my upper body strength at inpatient rehab, I was discharged home. Mom loaded up a luggage cart of the clothes, toiletries, and blankets I accumulated in my six-week stay and wheeled me out to our car, waiting at the front door of the lobby. On our drive home, Mom had to push me upright again after riding the curve of Lower Wacker and after any turn we took. Driving against oncoming traffic still felt like a game of Chicken, but we made it home.

That evening, Molly followed Dad and I up the stairs for the first time since my injury. Dad stabilized my hips as I gripped the smooth, unfinished body of the extra railing he installed for me earlier in the week. Carpeting squished underneath my tennis shoes as I slowly stepped my right foot up. I squeezed the railing as Dad helped my left leg catch my right.

One down, thirteen to go.

In the bathrooms, Dad installed grab bars on both sides of the toilets. He replaced my regular shower head with a handheld one. For weeks, Mom was the one to use it as she helped to wash my hair and shave my legs while I sat in my shower chair.

Would I ever take a shower while standing, again?

Mom helped my bony, naked body transfer on and off my shower chair. She helped me dry off and got me dressed in the morning.

In bed, my first night home, I laid on a wedge in an attempt to mimic what I was used to- the angle of a hospital bed. The wedge wasn't the same, though. I wanted the buttons of my hospital bed. The dark, rolling waves of the lake outside my window. The constant motion of nurses in the hallway.

I thumbed the makeshift call light Mom and Dad gave me. It was a doorbell. I slept with the button and the bell sat in the hallway, near Mom and Dad's bedroom. If I felt the pressure of my bladder or needed to change position, I rang.

My mouth salivated as I laid in bed, watching the stillness of my shadowed ceiling. My stomach turned and cramped. Mom was taking me to my first session at Day Rehab the next morning. My new schedule called for six hours of therapy a day, Monday through Friday.

Who would help me to the bathroom? What if I had an accident? I graduated from wearing pull-ups to wearing regular underwear a few days before. Yet, Keesha prowled through my mind, threatening to put me in diapers again.

How would I get to each therapy session? Where would I put my lunchbox?

My bladder pushed on my lower abdomen. I pressed my thumb to the round, plastic button of the doorbell, listening to the melody of the bell play in the hallway; the first of four times I'd press my makeshift call light for help that night.

CHAPTER
FORTY-SEVEN

May 19, 2015

T HE NEW CLINIC was small, a third of the size of the hospital's gym. Music played from the boombox in the corner of the room, by the only two treadmills they had. Most patients sat in a wheelchair, like me. Others used a walker or cane to get around.

Would I be walking like them one day?

In every workable spot in the gym, there was a patient and therapist exercising. I was lying in the back corner of the room where cool, plastic cushioning spanned the double-wide plinth beneath me. The bags under my eyes were heavier, pulling on my lower lids even more than they had that morning. The ceiling tiles were covered with squiggly, black holes. Like worm holes.

Even though I woke her and Dad four times to help me to the bathroom in the night, Mom still sat perky on the spare doctor's stool beside my new therapist, Claire, as she sat in on my therapy for the day.

Claire pinched the frame of her glasses, pushing them back toward her face. She touched her hip to the edge of the plinth as she laid a hand towel beneath my weak, left arm. Even though that arm hadn't moved yet, she slid it out to the side like a T and told me to try pulling it back to my side. In the darkness of my eyelids, the image of my body remained still.

How did I do this before? What did it feel like?

I took a deep breath, pursed my lips, and squeezed my eyes tighter. Tension surged through my body, firing every muscle it could. My face warmed as I squirmed in place.

"Jen!" Claire squealed, "It's moving!"

What? Was she sure?

Skin rolled under my chin as I lifted my head from my pillow.

There it was! My arm. It was lying alongside my gray Hanes t-shirt

Drew bought for me while I was still in the hospital. My hand sat at the seam, clenched in a fist.

Claire slid my arm back to the T position we started in as she flattened the rippled edges of the towel. She set her hands in her lap and scooted to the edge of her doctor's stool. Her hands hovered around my arm the way a new mom does when she lets go of her baby for the first time. "Now pull," she said.

Again, my lips pursed and my body stiffened as I squeezed every muscle in hopes of hitting the right one. Claire clapped and cheered, "That's it! Pull, pull, pull."

Through the blur of my parting eyelashes, there it was. My arm was resting at my side, again.

"I'm not even touching you," Claire said, "This is all you." She pushed my arm back to its starting point, "Let's keep going."

"Wait," Mom said. She pulled her phone out of her Mary Poppins' bag. "I gotta get this on camera for Dad!"

CHAPTER
FORTY-EIGHT

June 15, 2015

MARY WAS MY nurse, everyone's nurse, at Day Rehab. She wheeled me into one of the exam rooms and shut the door, hushing the clamor of therapists and patients working in the gym at the end of the hall. Butterflies swarmed my stomach.

She reached to either side of my wheelchair and pressed down on the brakes, as I asked, "Will it hurt?"

"It shouldn't." She patted the exam table. "Let's get you up here."

Mary held my waist while I pushed up from my wheelchair and pivoted to sit on the exam table. She lifted my legs and laid me down like my old therapists used to do. She slipped on a pair of latex gloves and rolled my shirt up to my ribs, exposing the clear rubber tubing extending from my abdomen.

"Does your G-tube have a balloon or a stopper?"

"I'm not sure." The night my G-tube fell out, no one told me if the new one was anchored in my stomach with a balloon or rubber stopper.

Mary held an empty syringe to the opening of my G-tube. She drew back the plunger to suck air out of my tube. If the anchor was a balloon, the balloon would deflate and slide out the opening in my abdomen. Mary gently pulled on my tube, feeling its resistance. "It must be a stopper," she said. She placed one hand on my abdomen and pulled on the tube with the other. She palpated, feeling for the edge of the stopper. She pulled on my tube again, but harder. And harder. Until she gasped, and I felt the wind knocked out of me.

It was a balloon, still inflated. She pressed a square of gauze down on the bloody opening of my abdomen. "That had to hurt," she grimaced.

It did.

As the pain quickly passed, my body felt relieved. Having the foreign object, tubing, out of my body made me feel whole.

Mary wiped the blood off my abdomen and taped a patch of fresh gauze over my former G-tube site. She helped me back into my wheelchair and wheeled me into the lunchroom where I'd eat Real Food.

No more tube feedings for me.

CHAPTER
FORTY-NINE

July 7, 2015

I WAS SITTING at our kitchen table at home. A sheath of water droplets layered the sides of my spouted glass. Blended sweet potato and mixed berries made the protein shake a mauve hue. A handful of napkins was cradled in the curve of a wooden stirrup that came from a child's Western saddle back in the day.

Grandma Kray's kitchen gadgets hung on the wall opposite me; her metal icing pipe, a rusty food scale, ice-block tongs. Wooden cheese boxes sat on the shelf beside the manual hand mixer I used to play with as a kid. I liked the way it hummed as I wound its handle. The gadgets brought back her cool linoleum kitchen floor which slid under my socks Sunday mornings, the prick of the skeleton key's keyhole on the basement door, and the marriage of sugar and yeast brushing my nose. My smoothie wasn't much compared to the kolaches she made, but it would do.

I needed a napkin. I stretched as far as I could, waving my fingers toward the stirrup. My legs felt pinned to my chair. I was still too weak to stand and keep my balance without holding onto something. Lying cheek to cheek with the oak grain of our table, I finger-walked my hand a little bit further.

"Mom!" I shouted and listened to the stillness of the first floor. "Dad!"

Tools clanked in the garage. The Allman Brothers sang through our opened windows, "Lord, I was born a rambling man. Trying to make a livin' and doin' the best I can ...."

I sucked in and pursed my lips, reaching for the napkins that were now centimeters from my fingertips. "Mom!" I called again, "Mom!"

Where had she even gone? Damnit, the napkins were right in front of me. Why couldn't I just reach the stupid things? If I was the old me, I would've stood up or walked around the table to get one in a second.

Tears welled in my eyes as I shouted at God, Why did You do this?

Our thirty-year-old hardwood floor creaked with the patter of Mom's bare feet. "Honey, I'm sorry. I just ran upstairs for a minute." She rested her arm along the back of my chair, "What can I get for you?"

"A napkin please," I snapped, sounding more like, A nabgin blease.

Mom leaned across the table, pulled a napkin from the stirrup, and set it to my right. "Anything else I can get for ya?"

"No." I glared at the napkins.

Why couldn't I walk like I used to? Barefoot, in a tank-top and running shorts. I would grab food from the fridge, take a paper plate from the cabinet, and land at the kitchen table with my hands full. My tanned legs would bend up onto the chair, my toes would hang off the edge as I bit into a turkey sandwich.

Progress didn't happen as swiftly as I wanted it to. Now that I was living at home, I was doing the activities I used to but not in the same way. Going to the bathroom, getting dressed, eating, walking across the room. Nothing I did in a day was quick or easy.

Although there were times I wanted to drop-kick the turn my life had taken, deep down I knew the help I needed from Dad to climb the stairs at night gave us a little extra time to talk before bed. The hair-styling assist I needed from Mom to braid my hair each morning didn't cease to make us laugh as we admired my Alfalfa's—my short, post-brain surgery hair that was growing back, making me look like Alfalfa from *The Little Rascals*. I said to leave the hair alone because I thought it added character. The additional 45 minutes it took me to finish a meal, due to my dysphagia, gave me more time around the table with family and friends.

While I had no plans to continue needing this extra help, I learned the beauty of slowing life down. It was supposed to go by in the blink of an eye, anyway. So really, what was the rush?

CHAPTER
FIFTY

August 20, 2015

"To the left a little more, they look better staggered," I said as hot air seemed to steam from Drew's nostrils. He was standing on his couch, reaching across the shelves of knick-knacks commemorating each of our dates. A warm breeze slid around the surrounding skyscrapers and in through his patio door. The thought of looking over the patio railing made my knees weak. The echo of car horns and screeching bus tires bounced in my eardrums. I imagined the ghost of my heels clapping on the sidewalk as Drew and I gallivanted through the city, foolishly in love last winter.

Drew moved the small bowls of pottery we made on Valentine's Day, two weeks before my brain bleed. The grit on the pottery wheel burned the sides of my hands as I shaped each bowl. Ours were easy to tell apart. Mine had smooth, round edges. His had lop-sided, wavy edges, which irritated him.

He shuffled them on the shelf and looked back at me for approval.

The bowl was sitting in line with the candle jar, not staggered. Which wasn't what I meant. I felt like eggshells were poking under my feet as I asked, "Actually, can you please move it back?"

He slid the bowl back.

I sighed, biting my tongue. I still didn't like the arrangement. If only I could have stood on the couch myself, moving the knick-knacks around. Drew would get to relax, put his feet on the coffee table, watch TV, and wait for me to finish decorating. Other girls got to decorate their boyfriends' apartments. They got to pick color schemes, set up picture frames, and make each room smell pretty.

My skin crawled as I asked, "Can I please see it without the candle?"

"Jen. It's fine," he said. He moved a picture of us posing on the beach from our vacation to Florida last Christmas. The lake breeze flowed through the patio door again, twirling my loose strands of hair. Drew picked up the photo of us from my first Cubs game and lined it up with another candle as I sank quietly into my wheelchair.

Our lives continued to be more and more different from our peers. Going out to eat, we had to use the wheelchair ramp off to the side or in the back of the building instead of using the front entrance, like our friends could. The sight of my wheelchair, the asymmetry of my face, and the spasticity that slurred my speech was off-putting to others. Cashiers, office assistants, waitresses, asked Drew what I needed before asking me. I stopped drinking alcohol which made the bar scene less enticing. In public or at a friend's house, Drew helped me in the bathroom. On the weekends we were together, he helped me in and out of the shower. For the sake of time, he helped me get dressed. From my underwear to my socks and shoes. Before leaving the house, we double checked that we brought my medicine, which I would take four times per day, and a snack to eat with it.

There wasn't a part of me or the day that Drew and I didn't share. One summer day, we stopped for lunch at a sandwich shop along the river; the river we kissed by on our second date. We were sitting at a picnic table, people-watching, and had just finished eating when I said I had to go to the bathroom. I didn't think I'd be able to hold it long enough to make the trip back to his apartment, so Drew wheeled me up the grassy hill to the bathrooms he said he saw earlier.

They were port-a-potties.

My nose scrunched at the sight of them. I didn't want my wheelchair to roll through the germs of the double-wide, accessible, portable bathroom, but Drew insisted. "Don't let anything touch me," I commanded as my eye began twitching.

He rolled me into the plastic box of seafoam green walls, lit up by the high noon sun. When Drew slid the lock on the door, the scent of steaming hot urinal cake set in. My skin grew clammy as I closed my eyes, wishing I was elsewhere. Drew laid two strips of toilet paper on either side of the toilet seat. He grabbed my underarms and pulled me out of my chair. He unbuttoned my khaki shorts, shimmied them down to my knees, and lowered me onto the toilet seat. Instead of reaching for the grab bar, I clung to his arm.

Drew held out a handful of toilet paper. I quickly wiped, careful not to hit my hand on the toilet or catch a glimpse of the stewing, blue liquid beneath me.

"Don't let anything touch me," I reminded Drew as he grabbed my underarms and boosted my shaky legs to a stand. I gasped as the toilet paper from the seat stuck to my sweaty buns.

"Ew, ew, ew! Get it off of me!" I hooked my arm around his neck, pressing our chests together. He peeled the paper off my bottom. He pulled on the waist of my shorts as my knees began to buckle.

"Jen, stand up," he said.

I leaned into his shoulder and started laughing, letting my knees buckle further. My shorts stuck to my thighs. Drew pursed his lips as he tugged on my waistband. Beads of sweat glistened as they rolled down the sides of his forehead.

"Don't let anything touch me!" I cackled. Every pore of my body seeped with sweat from the hot, smelly plastic bin we were encased in. My hand pressed into the wet cotton on Drew's back, where sweat began to weep through his shirt. He pulled harder on the waistband of my shorts, which were caught under the curve of my bum-cheeks.

"Get me out of here!" I laughed.

He yanked up my pants and tossed me into my wheelchair. A blast of fresh air relieved me as he busted the port-a-potty door open, I lathered myself in the hand sanitizer clipped to my wheelchair and hoped we'd never have to do that again.

"I need a shower," I said as Drew brought us back to the river walk.

The physical demands of our relationship were tiring and excluding at times. But not every couple was as blessed as we were to have memories as unique as the ones we made together.

CHAPTER
FIFTY-ONE

August 25, 2015

A T THE DAY Rehab clinic, wheelchairs crisscrossed through the gym as patients and therapists paired off to start their therapy sessions. I sat along the perimeter of the room, waiting to see which therapist would come.

The wheels of a standard, aluminum walker glided toward me, parking beside my right tire. In its silver frame stood Norma. She was 97 years old and couldn't weigh much more than that, either. She enclosed her cool hand around mine. The skin around her knuckles was puckered, pinched like the edges of pie crust. A metal cross hung from the silver necklace centered on her chest. She prayed before lunch every day, making the sign of the cross before and after her silent prayer. I wanted to bow my head and pray like she did, but what would others think? I wished I'd be as faithful as she was, one day.

"Hi Norma," I said.

Her eyes were glassy, filled with tears. She told me how well I was doing in therapy, how I would get all of my function back if I continued to work as hard as I was. She patted the back of my hand. "You are just beautiful. Especially your eyes," she said. "They're unusual."

She kept my hand cradled against her belly as she looked around the gym. Her soft smile, still intact as her therapist approached. "Hey, what do we have goin' on here?" A badge labeled PT hung from her neck as she tucked her laptop under her arm.

"Oh," Norma patted my hand, "I'm just telling Jen how beautiful she is."

"Aw," her therapist laughed. She tilted her head my way, "She is a beauty, isn't she? What do you say we get to physical therapy?"

Norma nodded, letting my hand slip from hers. She gripped her walker. Every few steps Norma stopped, turned her head to talk to her therapist, then looked forward and walked, again. Her cropped pants teased the heel of her slip-on shoes as she shuffled away.

My vision bounced, shaking the room up and down at all times. The right half of my face lay flat and my eye was fixed inward. My head rested off center, tilted to the right. My left shoulder drooped, which wasn't helped by my slumped posture. I didn't feel aesthetically appealing, but she saw something in me. Hopefully, it was God's light. I certainly saw it in her.

In the center of the gym, a dish towel hung from the clenched teeth of a girl in a wheelchair. Her arms were spastically curled into her chest. Her blue eyes bulged from their sockets like large marbles. Her head turned robotically as her big eyes scanned the room. Her body was often bent into some sort of incalculable position. One time I saw her leg raise to the front of her forehead as she bent sideways over the armrest of her wheelchair.

A beanpole of a boy waddled his way throughout the gym every day. His limbs looked wobbly and uncoordinated. A thin line of drool dripped from the corner of his mouth at all times, which he used his sleeve to wipe away when he remembered. His face looked bored like he wasn't registering his environment, unless he smiled. The light which radiated from his smile made it obvious he was cognitively aware, but only groans and grunts left his lips.

Unusual. Beautiful.

FIFTY-TWO

August 26, 2015

I WAS SITTING in my wheelchair, picking at the seal of the plastic bag Dad put my medicine in for lunch that day. Other patients pulled up to lunch tables around me in their wheelchairs and with their walking devices. A few others landed at my table, unzipping their lunch boxes and asking how therapy went that morning. A new patient rolled up to the open space beside me.

"Hi, I'm Emily," she said, waving to the patients around our lunch table.

"Hi," the four of us chimed before we laid the litany of Newcomer questions on her. "What's your diagnosis? How long were you in the hospital? Are you going back to work?" And so on.

I sipped my smoothie while they talked. Mom put together my lunch every morning, tossing sweet potato and berries in a blender. Even once I was approved to eat crunchy foods, I brought a smoothie to lunch. Having dysphagia meant there were precautions I had to take while eating, such as taking small bites and sipping water after each swallow of food. This made me a painfully slow eater. So, I stuck to smoothies.

Emily had a veggie sandwich, which was something I would have had if I chewed faster and swallowed better. Did she not like meat either? She was 27, a few years older than me.

"I had a brain bleed, in my brainstem," she said.

My body tensed.

"I haven't had surgery because the doctor said it was too dangerous of a spot to intervene."

That was what my on-call doctor told Mom and Dad.

I fingered through the side pocket of my backpack hanging on the back of my wheelchair. My cheeks warmed as my heart sped up. Where was my phone? Did we need to call 911? I asked, "Should we get help?"

She waved me off as she said, "Oh, no. The bleed stopped."

Stopped?

Emily was sitting in a wheelchair similar to mine. One of her eyes was opened wider than the other, like mine, but her voice sounded normal. Both of her arms moved like normal. With both hands she could open her lunchbox, hold her sandwich, reach up to fix her hair. She had a strong core, good posture. She could lean side to side, forward and back without losing her balance. She didn't run out of breath when she talked, either.

Why would God stop her bleed and not mine?

This question ate at me for the rest of the week.

That Monday, Mom wheeled me into the clinic for an early morning appointment with the doctor before therapy began. It was dark and rainy outside. The days were getting shorter, and the weather was getting cooler. I put the waiver for the adaptive camping trip Tom was going to take me on in my lap and under the weight of my weak hand. I needed the doctor's signature.

With a quick check of my vitals and a brief overview of the camping trip, my doctor signed the waiver. Mom opened the door of the doctor's office and began to push me out the door, but quickly stopped at a passerby. It was Emily. She was out of her wheelchair. Upright, walking into the clinic with a hemi-cane.

You had got to be shitting me, Jesus.

Mom wheeled me into the hallway, following behind Emily whose mom walked alongside her. I softened my glare when her mom turned around to apologize for them walking so slowly in front of us.

"Oh please, take your time." Mom said, "She looks great!"

The half-smile I gave hardly masked the growling green monster overtaking my insides.

Emily had been at the rehab clinic for one week and she had already ditched the wheelchair. I had been there for three months and still had to use a wheelchair to get from the parking lot to inside the clinic. She was walking tall with even strides down the hallway, focused on her balance.

As we neared the gym, I felt bad for envying her progress.

With a pouting lip I prayed, I'm sorry. Please continue to heal her.

Emily graduated from Day Rehab a few weeks later. She left using the hemi-cane to walk, without needing supervision. I now sincerely hope she made a full recovery and is living the life God called her to.

Later that night, my back bones jutted out from my naked body as I sat, slumped on the edge of my shower chair. Tears rolled down my lopsided face. The shower tile echoed my blubbery cry. Mom closed the toilet lid and sat down. She leaned toward me, asking, "Honey, what's wrong?"

"I feel distanced from God. I miss how close I was to Him in the ICU. The more progress I make, the more able I become, the less present He is in my mind. I used to depend on Him for every breath, but now I can multitask. I can brush my teeth without having to focus on brushing my teeth. I can put on my shirt without having to pray about keeping my balance. I don't depend on Him every moment of every day anymore. I feel like a toddler reaching up for her dad to carry her, but he wants her to walk instead."

Mom said, "God doesn't need to carry you anymore. He wants you to walk with Him." Her eyes were glassy as she watched my half-limp body sink further as I cried. "If I could take this on for you, I would," she said.

My tears suddenly stopped. "No!" This journey was mine. No matter how painful my suffering was, it brought me closer to God. I didn't want anyone to take that away from me.

I sat back in my shower chair, waited for Mom to turn on the shower, and carried on.

FIFTY-THREE

September 16, 2015

H AND GESTURES FLEW through the air, fingers pointed left and
right, stakes clanked into the ground as Tom directed the surrounding campers to set up tents. His combat boots marched through the
grass. His pocketknife clung to the back pocket of his jeans, brushed by
the hem of his black t-shirt. The corner of my lip pulled back like a half
moon. I relaxed into my wheelchair.

"All campers," a leader called with one hand cupped around his lips
and the other waving in the air. "Head down to the river!"

My head wobbled as Tom grabbed hold of the handles on the back of
my wheelchair and pushed me through the grass, onto the paved road,
and into the herd of campers rolling alongside us. Their bodies weaved
forward and back as their arms pumped like steel engines propelling their
own wheels.

They were so independent.

We turned at the end of the road. The sun flickered on the water, illuminating the trees as I counted kayak after kayak waiting along the boat-
launch. My arms itched to paddle, to push through the resistance of the
water. My core squeezed as I imagined weaving the oar side to side. My
legs tightened, wanting to stand from my wheelchair and slip into the tan-
dem kayak waiting for us.

Tom and a crew of volunteers guided my feet into the kayak, sitting
me down and strapping my weak hand to the oar handle. Tom hopped in
the seat behind me.

Pavement scraped the bottom of our kayak as volunteers pushed us
into the river, sending us gliding across the water. My seat cooled. Water
lapped against the sides of our kayak. Our herd of campers were already
approaching the turnaround down the river as I stroked my oar through

the water for the first time. Droplets danced, stretching and rolling their way up the paddle. Ripples scattered across the water's top. Lily pads laid over one another, brushing the sides of our kayak. The sun rolled in and out from behind puffy, cumulus clouds. My chin tilted back as sun rays cupped the sides of my face.

The other campers were shrinking as they paddled farther and farther down the river. "Hey, Jen," Tom said. "Let's catch up to them."

"Nah, that's okay." I shrugged, "Don't worry about it."

My weak hand, wrapped in the neoprene glove, slipped down the oar. I pulled at its Velcro strap. "This thing is just a little too loose."

"No, Jen." He insisted, "We're gonna catch up." His oar plowed through the water, making a breeze to play with my loose strands of hair. "You gotta be part of the group!"

What?

My shoulders turned inward as I wanted to shrink away. Staying back, in our own kayaking bubble, felt safer.

Since when was Tom the social one?

I dipped my oar side to side, wondering what kind of creatures my paddle was sweeping by. Our kayak began to rock as my paddling grew out of sync with Tom's.

Lurking beneath the surface of the dark water could've been the five-foot archaic vampire fish I saw on an episode of *River Monsters*. It had a creepy face, sort of flat like a catfish. It had a slimy, double set of dorsal fins. Goosebumps dotted my arms.

Yuck.

"Hey Jen," Tom said.

I turned my head to give him an ear. "Yeah?"

"You can stop paddling," his flat tone made this less of an offer and more of a command.

"Are you sure?"

"Yeah, don't worry about it," he said as I balanced the oar over my lap.

The loose hairs around my face became livelier, whipping around in a stronger breeze.

We must have been covering twenty meters per second. Was there a motor in this thing?

The night was beautiful, sitting under the stars. I stared, mesmerized by the crackles and flickers dancing in our campfire. Another young stroke survivor sat to my left and Tom was sitting on the tree stump to my right. Bags of marshmallows passed from camper to camper. Tom grabbed a stick and stuck a marshmallow on its end, holding it at the top of the fire for me.

Smoke curled and weaved into the night sky. Stars veiled its giant dome of darkness. Tom turned toward me with a golden-brown toasted marshmallow. "Jen, did you want a graham cracker or chocolate?"

Saliva streamed the insides of my cheeks. My fingers gravitated to the gooey, drooping 'mallow.

Oh yeah.

It clung to my fingers as I shimmied it off the stick "Um ... no, thanks," I said as I took a bite.

The melted, white goo stuck to my lips and smudged across my chin.

The survivor on my left had thick-framed glasses. His head tilted like mine, but he could move both of his arms. He squeezed a toasted 'mallow between two graham crackers as he quizzed Tom about his life, as if to figure out what it takes to be him. It was endearing and confusing at the same time.

Again, since when was Tom the social one?

As my gooey marshmallow coated my fingers and lips, my eyes shifted right to left trying to keep up with their conversation. What was so compelling about Tom's lifestyle?

My fellow survivor paused his conversation with Tom to lean toward me as he asked, "Do you need a napkin?"

My cheek puffed out, filled with the marshmallow as I answered, "Oh, no, I'm fine. Thanks."

Despite my decline, he insisted. His eyes lit up when Tom pulled a bandana out of his back pocket for me. I grabbed the blue handkerchief and wiped it across my face.

The next morning, crisp, cool air filled my nostrils as I opened my eyes to the top of our dew-covered tent. I pushed my sleeping bag cover off and exclaimed, "Good morning," to Tom.

It was hand cycling and rock climbing day!

After having breakfast among the pines, Tom wheeled me to the dead-end road, where a trailer of bikes was parked.

Tom helped the volunteer transfer me to a bike. It was low to the ground with footrests and hand pedals. The volunteer pulled out a roll of elastic bandage and wrapped my left, weak hand to the pedal to stabilize.

The other campers had use of both arms and took off on their hand bikes. Tom rode on a regular bike beside me, pushing the back of my bike to give me a boost. I was the caboose of the bike squad. When I pedaled, my bike veered to the left since my right arm was the only one actually pedaling.

The volunteers followed us on their bikes. Tom boosted me up a hill

until we reached a smooth, flat stretch of road. My tires veered to the left, toward the grassy edge leading down to a marsh.

The young, brunette volunteer had been riding with Tom and I. Her silky ponytail swung along her back as she giggled and tried to make conversation with Tom. Then, her bubbly voice welled up behind me, asking, "Jen, how about a boost?"

"Sure," I said.

She rode up behind me, saying, "When I push, you pedal. Ready?" She held the back edge of my seat and cheered, "Go!"

I pushed hard with my right hand, veering left and pedaling my bike right off the side of the road. Grass and rocks flew under my tires as I blazed down the hill. My head bounced side to side. My front tire caught a bump, throwing me into the ditch of cat tails and prairie grass.

Facedown in the bed of grass, I prayed, Please still let my arm be attached, please still let my arm be attached.

The volunteers came running down the hill. Helping me back on my feet, they walked me up to the road where my bike and the remaining campers were, with jaws wide open.

A volunteer— not the one who pushed me— sat me down on my bike and re-wrapped my hand to the pedal.

Tom waited beside me on his bike, looking as stunned as the other campers. I took hold of my other handlebar and said, "Don't tell Mom."

He nodded.

I was exhausted and ready to go back to bed upon our return to camp, but I couldn't. We had lunch and then headed to the event I'd been most looking forward to; rock climbing.

At the base of a sand-colored bluff, pine trees surrounded us like an amphitheater. Ropes, harnesses, and helmets sat on tree roots weaving in and out of the ground. The woods made it seem like there was no other world beyond what we had right then, no other world worth knowing, anyway.

Volunteers looped ropes and snapped metal clips together. They buckled their helmets and turned toward our group, asking, "Who wants to go first?"

Before my arm could raise, a dull, pressure squeezed my head. My muscles tightened. My body began to ache. Another camper raised his hand, taking on the first climb. One of the volunteers was helping him into a harness when the ache in my body grew deeper. The pain in my head squeezed tighter as my morning bike crash replayed in my mind.

Our group leader was leaning on the tree beside Tom. I touched my palm to the side of my head and looked their way, saying, "I have a headache."

Our group leader asked, "Do you think you're dehydrated?" She held her water bottle up, saying, "I know I haven't been drinking enough."

Chills ran up my spine as the morning Dad and I were hunting filled my mind. We had been walking the snow-covered cornfields when a gust of wind slapped my cheek.

"Jen, stay with us," Dad called back to me.

I tried marching my heavy boots a little higher, a little faster, to catch up. My head ached and squeezed in pain. I thought I needed some water, that I was dehydrated.

I stared at the splintered pieces of wood chips covering the ground. "No," I said, trying to remember how much water I'd been drinking.

What if I was having another stroke?

Another camper, sporting a French manicure and a perfectly tousled low bun under her baseball cap, reached into her purse hanging from the side of her wheelchair. She pulled out a small, white bottle, saying, "I have some ibuprofen, if you want?"

My mind raced back to the moment I was standing in the kitchen at our lake house. I was taking the pill Mom gave me to ease my headache before Dad and I left to go hunting.

"It's sitting on the counter," she said from the hallway.

"Oh, yeah. I see it," I said. There was a blue pill sitting on the kitchen counter next to the travel-size bottle of Aleve. I raised my voice, saying, "Thanks," hoping she heard me as I tossed it in my mouth and took a swig of water. I leaned over the counter with my head in my hands.

"Jen, are you ready?" Dad asked, carrying our shotguns to the door. "We gotta go."

"Yeah," I stood up and walked towards the door, kissing Mom on the cheek as I passed by. Each of us talked over the other, saying, "Okay, bye!"

"Bye!"

"Bye!"

"Bye!" And the worn-out screen door shut behind us.

The pretty girl in the wheelchair tilted her head as tears filled my eyes.

This couldn't be happening. Someone needed to call Dr. Baskaya.

My heart pounded as the surrounding pine and bluffs began to close in.

"I can't do this," I whispered to Tom.

Tears streamed down my face.

Tom leaned toward me. His voice lowered as he asked, "Do you want to go back?"

I glanced at the sea of wood chips beneath us. The volunteer-climbers tossed piles of ropes to the side and tied knots in others. A volunteer's dog lumbered his big paws around the grounds as the first camper scaled up the side of the bluff. Rock climbing was the activity I had most looked forward to.

If I left, I'd feel like a wimp.

The pain in my head squeezed tighter. My stomach sank.

What if I was having a stroke?

Suddenly, the Day Rehab lobby flashed in my mind. The one I walked through every weekday morning at 8:20 a.m. Six hours a day, five days a week I worked in that clinic, trying to get better. The coming week would be no different.

"Yeah," I sighed.

Tom helped me back to camp. That afternoon, he and I relaxed, snacked, and played a game of Bags while my headache subsided. We had another campfire that night and headed home the next morning. Despite the struggles, it was the best weekend I'd had.

Thank you, Tom, for being the best big brother around. I feel incredibly blessed.

CHAPTER
FIFTY-FOUR

October 13, 2015

MOM RUSHED ME in my wheelchair, into a classroom of aspiring occupational therapists.

"Hi! We're here!" I said. I waved and slapped my hand to my thigh to catch the sheets of notes sliding off my lap. The clock read 12:56 pm, four minutes before my presentation was to begin.

The title page of my PowerPoint was lit up on the overhead screen. *My Story*, it read. Mom parked me to the side of the overhead screen. My old neuroscience professor clipped a bug-sized microphone to the floral scarf hanging loosely around my neck. I shuffled my notes together as the little mic fell to my lap. My professor re-clipped it to my scarf as the room full of tired graduate students watched it tumble to my lap, again.

"Mom, why don't you sit next to me and hold the microphone instead?"

A student rolled a wheely chair over for Mom to sit in as I listened to my professor introduce me to her class. A young woman was taking notes at my old desk. Her navy V-neck shirt framed the silver necklace on her chest. Her hair was twisted into a bun. Her backpack sat on the floor in the same slouched position mine used to. A cluster of my old classmates and professors filled the back wall.

"Hi," I said. "My name is Jenny and I'm here to share my story." *My story*, an underwhelming title, but what title could possibly suffice?

Last year's photos filled the first PowerPoint slide. My smile was full, symmetrical. My body was balanced and strong; walking, running, standing. My arms hugged friends, held a freshly caught bluegill, and hung onto Molly's collar. Those memories cut off at the switch to the next slide. The word Cavernoma sat next to an image of tangled blood vessels I copied and pasted from Google.

"It's about the size of a raspberry," I said. My nose scrunched at the bump of the microphone hitting my chin. Mom held her arm out like a car model, keeping her gaze on the students and smiling as she pushed the microphone between my lips.

I pointed at the next slide covering the screen. "In this photo, we're working on sitting at the edge of the bed." I continued as the round, foam top of the microphone grazed my nostrils.

Mom.

I leaned back, giving myself a double chin as I dodged her hand, but she followed my mouth with the microphone. A few students jotted notes in spiral notebooks, one girl stared at the cellphone hidden behind her binder, and the rest kept their eyes on the overhead screen. A new slide flashed to a photo of me on a treadmill. "So, once I got to Inpatient Rehab," I said as Mom's breath warmed my neck.

"Tell them about Georgia," she whispered.

What? That had nothing to do with what I was talking about.

Georgia was the hospital therapy dog that I played fetch with a couple of times. She was a big, black Labradoodle who eased my longing for Molly and was choosy about which commands she followed.

The microphone brushed my chin, again. My eyes slowly shifted as I scanned the room, hoping not to see any confused faces, any smirks or grins entertained by Mom's assistant work. Especially in the first row, arm's length away.

"I spent a year in Day Rehab. Five days a week, six hours a day."

Mom kept her eyes on the audience as she leaned into my shoulder, trying not to move her lips. "Tell them about the time Big Mike picked you up," she said.

Her pride for my public speaking and the progress I'd made in my recovery radiated in her smile, but did she know they could *see* her? And I already planned out what I was going to say today. Why she saved her requests for the actual presentation and offered none for the practice presentations I performed for her and Dad was a wonder.

I glanced at my notes as they slid from my fingers and rose to my chin. "So you can see better," Mom whispered.

What was she doing? My belly tightened to hold in a burst of laughter as she pushed the microphone into my nose, again.

The last slide flashed on the screen. Mom resisted me as I pulled my notes back to my lap. Scribbles and arrows surrounded the miniature slide printed on my paper as Dr. Dhawan's voice stung my ears, You're having a brain bleed.

"When I was in the E.R.," I said, "I knew there was a chance I could die. I knew there was a chance this might be my last day. Not once did I think about my jean size, what work had been like that week, or about being stuck in traffic the day before. The one and only thought I had was, had I given enough to others? I was terrified at twenty-three I had not given enough. I had not given to God or done anything yet. My life was about me. Sure, I picked a profession to help others, but at the end of the day my life was about me."

The corner of my lip pulled to my cheek as scenes of my recovery played in my head. "Moving forward, I encourage you to be a student of life. Be prepared to learn from people in your field, people who are more experienced than you, like your supervisors; equally experienced, like your classmates and co-workers; and less experienced, like your patients and their caregivers. You can learn from anyone. Keep your curiosity alive. Ask questions, read books, watch movies, be with nature, draw, play games, do whatever you need to never stop learning.

"Finally, I want to share my firm belief that no one story is more impressive than the other. A loss is a loss. There are many more miracles you will meet along your way. I happen to have this unique opportunity to share my story with you today. Thank you."

FIFTY-FIVE

THE DAY BEFORE Thanksgiving, the rehab gym smelled of roasted turkey, mashed potatoes, and buttery casseroles. There were two long tables filled with dishes us patients and therapists brought in. I brought the Oreo and candy corn cookies Mom had crafted to look like turkeys.

When Drew walked through the sliding doors, my heart tingled and the butterflies in my stomach tickled the way they did every time I saw him. He was put together, as if he could be in some sort of preppy, timeless magazine ad. Whenever he walked toward me, in public or at home, I forgot about the other people around us.

He had the day off work and came to join us patients for the feast. He wheeled me through the food line, helping me make a plate of a little bit of everything. We sat in the back corner of the lunchroom at a table with one of the youngest patients at the clinic. She was battling a rare, degenerative neurological disorder which left her nonverbal and uncoordinated. From what I saw, her mom never left her side. She came to every one of her therapy sessions and activities, including this Thanksgiving feast.

Drew and I gushed to them about our plans to move into his apartment together. I never wanted to live with anyone before I was married, but I knew I would marry Drew. Since I would need physical help around the house, it only made sense to live together first. He was renting an apartment in the next town over. It was on the first floor, had enough room to get around in a wheelchair or with my walker, and had an attached garage. We wouldn't have to worry about me getting in and out of the car in bad weather or jockeying for a close parking spot.

"I'll move in once this is all over," I said as I waved my hand in the air, referring to rehab and my disabled body. Drew and I knew I'd make a full recovery.

The young patient's mom paused. She cracked a smile and furrowed her eyebrows. "You know this is never really over, right?"

CHAPTER
FIFTY-SIX

IT WAS EARLY spring 2016 when we started cutting my hours of ther-apy back at the Day Rehab clinic. My progress was slowing. I no longer needed the daily intervention of rehab when my body wasn't changing every day. Instead of being at the clinic five full days a week, I attended three. This change was also in preparation for my discharge and transition to outpatient therapy.

Mom, Dad, and I went to the lake house one of those spring weekends. We had been back to the lake house before, but even the first time back wasn't as overwhelming as I thought it would be. Still, each time we went, the morning of my brain bleed replayed in my head as Dad helped me through the creaky, front screen door. We walked the hallway where our boots squeaked from melting snow. I stood in front of the bathroom mir-ror recalling my confusion as my arm began losing function. I sat in the recliner I was in moments before I collapsed and Dad yelled for Mom to call 911. While every detail was fresh in my mind, my years of happy memories at the lake house outweighed my one, traumatic memory.

At the time of this spring weekend, I was walking independently with a platform walker. I was still wearing the same rigid leg brace, or AFO, I had from the inpatient rehab hospital to manage my drop foot. My left arm was still lagging behind the rest of my body, in the way of progress. My arm had minimal movement. It was helpful for stabilizing objects during activities like putting toothpaste on my toothbrush. Otherwise, I consid-ered it still asleep.

I had it propped up on the kitchen table when I asked Mom and Dad why the doctor waited to do my brain surgery until the day after my bleed started. They paused. Mom sat down at the table. Dad stood behind her.

Mom began, "After you were flown from the emergency room, you arrived at the university hospital about 3:30 pm that Saturday." The day Dad and I were out hunting. "You were admitted to the Neuro ICU, alert and oriented, where residents confirmed you were having a brain bleed. A pontine-medullary hemorrhage. The on-call surgeon didn't come to the hospital. Over the phone, he told the fifth-year resident who was taking care of you, that the location of your bleed was inoperable, too dangerous to intervene. He said the only option was to observe you.

"Through the evening, you deteriorated rapidly. The bleed got bigger and bigger," Mom said. "You became disoriented, unable to respond to questions, and eventually lost consciousness. You were sick and aspirating on your vomit. They intubated you, put you on a ventilator. You had no spontaneous respiration and your heart rate dropped to the 20's and 30's.

"At your bedside, they drilled a burr hole into the top of your head to relieve the pressure off your brain. The next morning, the on-call surgeon came in for his regular shift. He saw you for the first time. He told me, Dad, Drew, and Tom that you probably wouldn't survive the day. The team put a PICC line in to make you more comfortable."

Dad looked away as she continued, "That afternoon, the skull base neurosurgeon was walking through your unit. He was done with work, heading home for his daughter's birthday party when he saw you. He started asking the nurses questions. He wanted to know who you were, what happened to you, why had no one called him? If he didn't do anything, you were going to die. He quickly called his daughter. He told her there was a girl at the hospital who needed his help, but if he helped, he wouldn't be able to make her birthday party. His daughter said, 'It's okay Papa, go save her life.'

"I was standing outside of your room when the team began packing up your ventilator. I asked if they were taking you somewhere. One of the nurses said a different surgeon was taking over your case. Another nurse ran to get your dad, who was praying in the chapel on the other side of the hospital. The surgeon said he didn't know what he'd bring back or who he'd bring back, but he thought you deserved a chance. Then, he took you to surgery.

"He came back with you four hours later. We had to wait until the next morning to see if you'd wake up. Dad, Drew, Tom and I spent the night in your room and the next morning Dad and Drew came to your bedside. When they called out your name, you opened your eyes and two tears ran down your cheek."

My jaw hung open. My hand waved as I asked, "But what about the on-call surgeon? Why didn't he come sooner? Why didn't he call the skull base neurosurgeon before?"

Dad's voice cracked as he answered, "The bastard never showed, Jen."

All breath seemed to escape me.

My brain bleed didn't have to be as severe as it was. I didn't have to be as disabled as I was.

A pit began to hollow my stomach. Tears filled my eyes.

Suddenly, God seemed powerless, miniscule.

Why wouldn't He have intervened sooner?

CHAPTER
FIFTY-SEVEN

July 30, 2017

I HAD BEEN out of Day Rehab for two months. I was going to outpatient therapy three times per week, but Dad and I kept my six-hour therapy schedule going at home. Our living room served as our main gym. The wooden coffee table, which creaked and shifted under the weight of my body, was our makeshift plinth. While I laid on my back, Dad assisted my arm as I tried reaching up and down. We worked on speech therapy at the kitchen table. I practiced saying ten-word sentences in one breath and pronouncing words starting with M, B, or P. My facial palsy kept my lips from curling under and pressing together to make those sounds. On the big rug in our living room, bruises spotted my kneecaps from our kneeling exercises and my feet ached after our repetitions of standing. My therapy goal was to stand for two minutes straight, but the buckling of my knees and my poor balance made it a fight.

My progress continued to slow. The measures we used to track my progress, such as degrees of motion or the number of feet I walked, were no longer changing. I had to trust in the subjective markers of simply feeling as if my arm was moving a little more or seeming to look stronger as I walked. I had been using the platform walker for over a year. My left arm still had minimal movement, I needed an AFO to walk, my vision still jumped and swayed constantly, I had high tone and spasticity, especially in my jaw, and my voice still had a strange, hyper-nasal tone to it.

I was lying on the big rug in the living room with Dad stabilizing my knees as I arched my hips in the air. My body angled down, drooping to the weaker, heavier side when I tried. After the second set I dropped my hips to the ground. "I cannot stand doing one more repetition of one more exercise," I snapped.

I couldn't sit up or get off the floor on my own. Half of my body was strong enough to stand and the other, weak half felt pinned to the ground.

Why couldn't I be normal?

"Will you take me to church?" I demanded more than I asked. I wanted to look God in the face, to be in His own house while He explained the good reason for letting this happen to me.

Dad helped me into the garage. I sat on the edge of the passenger seat while he lifted my legs into the car. He scooched me back and pulled my seatbelt across my body before walking around to the driver's side. The engine grumbled when he turned the ignition. I clenched my jaw to hold back tears as we sat in silence. He slowly pulled out of the driveway. Subdivisions of two-story homes rolled across my car window. Dad took a left at the forest preserve as we did every Sunday to go to church. My shoulders wound tight as I thought about barging through those front doors.

My bum foot caught on the carpeted aisle I used to walk down so easily to receive Communion as a kid. Dad grabbed my hips when my cane tipped onto two of its four feet. Rows of empty pews sat in the bit of daylight peeking through the ceiling windows. And there was Jesus, the near life-size statue of Him hanging on the cross above the altar.

I screamed inside, You!

Jesus' face looked on as if looking over the congregation. His fingers were curled towards the nails hammered into his hands. Tension burned in my arm as I readied to throw my cane at Him, but I couldn't. I needed the damned thing to walk. I slammed its four peg feet into the ground with each step.

You did this! And for what?

My left arm flopped against my side as I swung my leg to step forward. My knees weakened at the first step of the altar. "Just leave me here," I told Dad.

He lowered me to the ground, letting my legs fold beneath me as I pulled my limp arm onto the step, burying my face in my hands. The side of my mouth smeared saliva onto my forearm as I sobbed. Tears seeped into the corners of my mouth, salty on the sides of my tongue. Mucus oozed from my nostrils, dripping across my upper lip. My chest pumped back and forth, blowing short puffs of air in and out of my mouth. My words bellowed through my insides as I demanded answers.

Why did You do this?

The more my spasticity pulled my jaw to the side, the more I noticed the dead half of my face. The more my spasticity pulled at my arm, the more I noticed the spasms in my trunk. The more I noticed, the more handicapped I felt, and the more I cried.

As I lay hunched over the bottom step of the altar, a big, steady breath suddenly blew into my lungs. Then, another. My belly softened and my chest sank into the hardwood of the altar step. My shoulders relaxed and my refuse of tears puddled on my eyelashes.

Dad was sitting in the third pew back, staring at the crucified Jesus when I raised my voice to him. "Okay," I said with my head still buried in my arms.

Dad walked over. He tucked his hands under my armpits and pulled me to my feet. I used his hand as a cane to walk back to the pew. My bottom plopped onto the cushioned bench, letting my spine slump into the wooden back as Dad put his arm around me.

Jesus was still hanging on the cross in the same spot He was when Dad and I walked in. His hands and feet were still pinned down by nails. His head was still crowned in thorns. His face dismayed, yet trusting. My body paralleled His body, resembling a human wreckage. Out of man's own selfishness and pride did our bodies become so broken. What a mystery it was, why my life had taken such a drastic turn. Even so, I couldn't deny the quiet, yet persistent voice telling me to trust.

PART III

CHAPTER
FIFTY-EIGHT

May 13, 2018

THE EGG-SHAPED OFFICE chair I begged Mom and Dad for in middle school was holding me at the desk in my bedroom. There was a pit in my stomach, different from the butterflies I had the first time I called Drew three and a half years before. The black screen of my iPad stared at me, waiting to be pressed and swiped, but once I did, I'd be one step closer to talking with Drew.

Mom, Dad, and I were driving home from a weekend at the lake house when my phone buzzed in the side door. It was a text from Drew. I slid my thumb across the screen to read, "Can I call you to talk?"

To talk.

My gut sank. The fields of muddy crops speeding by my window were suddenly mesmerizing. Either he cheated on me or he was going to break up with me. That was the case when any lover wanted to talk.

My finger swiped across my iPad as Drew's short temper filled my mind. Our last few phone calls were riddled with quick defenses and monotone answers. Last spring, I impulsively signed up to pursue a master's degree in chaplaincy. If I couldn't physically manage being an occupational therapist, I wanted to pursue something in the realm of faith. Getting a new master's degree eased my longing for the old one. I took one online course at a time. I craved the theological conversations I was having with other students online to be happening with Drew, offline. I sensed a barrier sprouting between us when I was studying the New Testament for the first time. Learning about the Beatitudes and how God calls us to a fuller life through chastity and obedience left me in awe. When I asked Drew his thoughts about chastity or Jesus, he said, "Don't worry about it, Jen," ending the conversation before it started. After my first year of classes, Drew became concerned that school was taking too much of my time.

He was more concerned about my rehabilitation. He thought I should be more focused on my recovery and that if it were him, he'd be working on his recovery "24/7." He didn't like Dad being the one to help with my at-home exercises every day. He wanted me to have a certified physical therapist to work at home with all day, even though such a service didn't exist. He seemed frustrated I wasn't doing enough, even though I didn't know what more I could possibly be doing. To ease his concern, I emailed the athletic trainer at the hospital. I studied bodybuilding websites. I talked with my physical therapists; but no resource was giving me the magic bullet to recovery that Drew seemed to want me to find. Before one of our last phone calls ended, my lips tightened when I said, "A negative attitude is far more limiting than my physical deficits would ever be."

Drew and I were also in the midst of renovating a condo near his work, an hour away from Mom and Dad. Drew wanted to make the condo accessible for me, although I didn't need many modifications. I requested no carpeting for ease of walking and grab bars in the bathroom. I didn't get the chance to live in his former apartment because his lease ended before I was finished with therapy. I was still hesitant to live with anyone before I was married, but Drew reminded me of how our circumstances were different. While I could walk household distances with a cane, I was still at risk for falling. Having lower physical energy and only one functional arm, I could use the extra help with house chores. Some of our friends were already living with their boyfriends and girlfriends. Not to mention, Drew and I were planning on getting married, anyway.

So, I gave in. We set a date to move in together in January 2018, but I was still attending outpatient therapy near Mom and Dad. My discharge date was pushed back month after month as I continued to make progress. The extensions were a good thing. Only the patients who were progressing got extended therapy, but I wanted to get going on life with Drew. Come May, I had a final discharge date set for the end of the month. Less than two weeks after my video call with Drew.

Despite this past tension, I smiled while I sat among the tune of my iPad's ringtone, waiting for Drew to answer my call. When his face filled the screen, a tear rolled down his cheek.

I gasped, "What's wrong?"

"We need to take a break." Another tear rolled down his cheek. He was wearing one of his plain t-shirts, made of the soft cotton I grabbed onto for a hug or kiss. He was sitting on the cream-colored couch we had picked out together, the one I thought made it obvious we didn't have kids yet. And the daylight lit up the room, beaming through the sliding doors in the living room and kitchen.

My gut dropped. Blood drained from my face as my jaw hung open. An imaginary wall rose between us, suddenly making us strangers instead of lovers. I leaned forward to catch my breath. "What?"

He said he wanted to be single. He wanted to live alone, stay up late—I was a strict nine pm-er—and be able to go out to the bars—I couldn't make out peoples' voices in noisy environments and the thought of navigating nightlife with a wheelchair seemed "too hard for us," as he would say. Not to mention, I no longer drank alcohol. He said he felt more like a caregiver than a boyfriend and that he was overwhelmed. Plus, we had only been dating a few months before my brain bleed happened. Over and over he said, "I'm not a good person, Jen."

I wailed. Tears streamed along the sides of my face, trailing my jawline and wetting my neck. Mucus smeared my face as I wiped my sleeve across my upper lip, soaking my shirt up to my elbow. I wanted to tell him I could stay up late, I could go to bars, I could do whatever he needed me to do. If we weren't together, he wouldn't be able to see my progress. We wouldn't be able to do things together, make memories. My heart ached. My chest felt like it was caving in as I said, "You're going to miss out."

He wiped his thumb under the corner of his eye. "I have to go" he said. "I'm really overwhelmed."

"No!" I cried, "Please don't go." I wiped my sleeve under my nose, smearing another glob of mucus across my cheek.

If he hung up, when would I see him again?

"I'm sorry. I'm really overwhelmed. I have to go."

"No, please don't go!"

When the camera went black, my body buckled at the waist.

How could God let this happen? Drew and I were supposed to be together. We were supposed to get married and have a family. How could God be all powerful if our plans were broken? He couldn't be. Did He even exist?

I gasped as a chill rushed over my body.

If I didn't believe in God, what did I have left? Myself?

I prayed, Fine, You're real, but I want nothing to do with You.

My heart felt like it was tearing in half, each fiber of muscle bursting at its seam. How was I still breathing? How could my heart still be beating under the pain it was in?

Take me, please take me, I begged God. I wouldn't be able to live like this, in this much pain and heartache. No one could. But if I was in Heaven, Drew would still be down on Earth. I for sure wouldn't be able to get back together with him, then.

I stopped begging. Dad knocked and slowly opened my bedroom door. He rushed to kneel at my feet when he saw my tears. He pushed my shoulders back to see my face. "Honey, what's wrong?"

"Drew bro—" my spasticity jerked my head to the side as my voice cracked into a screaming, high-pitched sob. "Drew bro—"

Dad repeated after my slurred, bellowing voice, "Drew. Broke. Up." I pointed at myself before buckling over, again.

Dad's eyes widened and turned glassy. "Drew broke up with you?"

I collapsed into his shoulder. My teeth rubbed against the stripes of his button-down shirt. Drool seeped out my open mouth. My arms were limp at my side as Dad held me. I hadn't stepped a single step of my new life without Drew in it. How would I even begin?

CHAPTER
FIFTY-NINE

L ATER THAT NIGHT, I was sitting in my wheelchair, beside my bathroom sink when Dad was helping me get ready for bed as he normally did; not because I needed help, but because he couldn't resist helping. He was putting toothpaste on my electric toothbrush, which he claimed was for lazy people, when I thumbed the promise ring Drew gave me after I got out of the hospital two summers ago. He said he wanted to marry me someday.

I pushed the gold band with my thumb nail but couldn't move it past my knuckle. My left arm was sitting lifelessly alongside me. My eyes welled with tears I didn't think I had left. I lifted the back of my hand toward Dad the way a newly engaged woman would, to show off her ring. He took my hand, putting his thumb and finger on either side of the gold band. The smooth metal slowly slid down my finger, taking my future plans with it. Dad put it in his pocket as I let out a sob, wiping tears with my newly bare hand.

The next morning, I seemed to shed an equal number of tears. My twenty-seventh birthday was a couple months away, I was single, disabled, unemployed, and living at home with Mom and Dad. I couldn't drive, I didn't have a social life outside of the one I had with Drew, and I quit chaplaincy school. With Drew thinking school was a distraction from my recovery and my new distaste for God, I dropped out.

Every inch of our house held a memory of Drew. The notepad on my bedroom shelf was the one he used to write me notes and leave on my pillow at night. When I gripped the stair railing, I remembered the way he lifted my weak foot to put on the next step for me. At every meal, I thought about what conversation he and I would be having or what comment he would make at the news anchor on TV. Near the laundry room was where he kicked off his shoes. The blueberry breakfast bars in the pantry were his favorite. Any moment of my day could be traced back to him.

My insides dwelled in a dull, constant pain, like I was rotting from the inside out. All the ways I might have derailed our relationship, with my insecurities and need for control, ruled my mind. In our daydreams of wedding planning, I wanted to get married in a church, but he wanted to get married on a beach.

If he knew I'd agree to get married outside, maybe he'd want to get back together.

I rushed to my iPad, staring into its screen until my eyes reddened as I planned a hypothetical wedding for us; one I thought he would want. I saved photos of white sand beaches and altars with canopies made of flowers and billowy linens. My top pick for a dress had a low-cut back and would follow the curves of my body, the way it did for the model online. A three-tiered key lime cake with buttercream frosting would be a hit for dessert.

My online research expanded to lace bras. I only wore shapeless, spandex sports bras from high school and college. Unless, an outfit like a cocktail dress demanded my wearing of a Real Bra. For Drew, pulling off my shirt to find an old, gray sports bra across my chest had to be underwhelming.

If he knew I switched to wearing Real Bras, maybe he'd love me again.

I emptied my dresser drawer, throwing all but one of my sports bras into a garbage bag. The next day, I wrestled with the clasp of a Real Bra. With my one, strong hand I brought the two bra ends together, sliding the hook over the clasp. The fabric sprung back as the hook and clasp missed. I tried again, bringing the two ends of fabric together with my thumb and pointer finger. The hook and clasp slid by each other. Missed again. For a third time I brought the fabric together, but now felt the latch of the little metal hook and clasp. After two days of repeating the dance between the hook and clasp, I summoned Mom to an errand at Victoria's Secret. I requested sexy sports bras that a mature, adult woman would wear. She restocked my dresser drawer with sports bras made with mesh, cut-out patterns, and scalloped edging.

If Drew knew I wore these new, sexier bras, maybe he'd want to get back together.

However, if my wedding plans and new bras were not enough, a tattoo could show I'd changed for the better. Drew had two of them. I didn't have any, but the way he looked at other women with tattoos made me want one. My online search expanded to body art. I saved pictures of small, feminine tattoos. I thought a delicate floral design was the right balance between girly-girl and rebel. Guys seemed to like tattoos on girls' hips. It was a sort of teaser or reminder to what's available below.

A hip tattoo, it was. In my collection of design samples, images of tattoo sleeves popped up. Collages of blossoms and buds, shaded to look as soft as they were in real life, decorated the arms of strong, sensual women. If Drew saw me like that, he'd be even more impressed. People with tattoos seemed bold and secure, like they knew who they were.

If I got a tattoo, or seven, maybe he'd want to get back together.

Toward the end of our relationship, I had pushed aside his urge for me to workout at a gym. I made small improvements every couple of weeks, which was nil compared to the gains I used to make daily. He assumed my plateau in recovery meant the exercises I was doing with Dad were not effective, therefore, slowing my progress. Drew wanted me to find an exercise and nutrition program that laid out the steps to achieving a full recovery. He told me, "There has to be someone who had what you had and made a full recovery. Find out how they exercised and ate, and then do as they did."

Drew had good intentions, but he didn't realize what he was asking of me. His focus on my full recovery was a reflection of his desire for our lives to go back to the way they were before my brain bleed. He didn't want me to suffer. He didn't want me to have to deal with walking devices, needing medication, or enduring the stigma of physical disability. I had a feeling he wanted to be back on our first date, roaming the snow-fallen city streets and dreaming of a future together. I wouldn't blame him.

Nonetheless, I thought if he knew I joined the gym maybe he'd consider getting back together. I told Dad my desire to lift weights had nothing to do with Drew, that the timing was a coincidence. Whether or not he believed me, Dad took me to the local gym three days per week.

The smell of tennis shoes and sweat filled my nose. Dad strapped my weak, left hand to the handlebar on the tricep machine. The ten-pound block of lead slid up a set of cables as I pushed the handlebar halfway. A fiery sensation ran up the backs of my arms. My face scrunched as I pushed. Dad pressed on the top of the left handlebar, helping me reach the full range. My elbows bent, easing the handlebars back to the start.

Twenty-nine to go.

We made a routine of doing the first twelve leg and arm machines, followed by core exercises and a round on the elliptical. The row machine became the encore exercise. After finishing the main routine, Dad set me up for rowing. He sat me on the small, square seat which glided forward and backward. I wore a glove that kept my weaker hand strapped in a grip around the handlebar. My feet sat in the footrests at the base of the machine where water swished in its round jug each time I pulled back the handlebar. Although Dad agreed to spot me as I slid back and forth on the machine, his eyes were glued to the flat screen TV's hanging from the ceiling. He said he would've caught me if need be, but I didn't hold my breath.

We were passing by those rowing machines one morning when I got a whiff of Drew's cologne. Even though he lived an hour away and had no reason to be at the gym, tears welled in my eyes as they darted through the room. He wasn't at the row of treadmills or the corner of dumb bells. He wasn't in the mix of people walking by, either.

If he wasn't at the gym, then who was the asshole wearing his cologne?

Familiar scents were not the only reminders of Drew. I was sitting on the bicep curl machine when a familiar beat triggered my first-date butterflies with him. The gym speakers boomed, "If you gave me a chance I would take it, it's a shot in the dark, but I'll make it ... no place I'd rather be ...."

It was a song from the mix CD Drew gave me on our first date. We were standing under the glow of a streetlamp, dwarfed by the surrounding skyscrapers, and in the hustle of city slickers when he pulled the CD case from his pocket.

"No place I'd rather be," the gym speakers sang.

I dropped the bicep handlebars and burst into tears. "Why did he leave me?"

Dad put his hand on my shoulder. "Come on honey," he said. "You'll be alright."

Another time, I was using the leg press when a Drew look-alike passed by. He had the same fair-skinned, sculpted arms framed by a cutoff t-shirt. The prickly shadow along his jaw was trimmed close like Drew's. My head dropped back. Tears streamed along my cheeks. Dad sat in my wheelchair, waiting for my memories to pass as he fought tears of his own.

The happenings of my relationship with Drew replayed in my mind constantly. Not only did I cry at the gym, but also during dinner with Mom and Dad, while getting dressed in the mornings, while at the grocery store, and as I went to sleep at night.

I needed a distraction. I needed to be social, but Drew was my best friend, my main social outlet. The majority of my friends lived out of state. The few who were local didn't have the time to fill my need to get out of the house or talk about Drew whenever I wanted. They had jobs, households of their own. Without Drew, I hardly had a life.

CHAPTER
SIXTY

May 27, 2018

I HAD SCOURED the internet in the days leading up to Mass, searching for meet-up groups in our west suburban town. Sewing club? No, thanks. Coffee Talk? Coffee was gross. Mom's lunch? Didn't have kids.

Drew would've found something by now.

I needed something close, so Mom and Dad didn't have to drive far to drop me off.

Our church was five minutes away. Although I wanted nothing to do with God, I was desperate to get Drew off my mind. The church bulletin was posted on our parish's website. Announcements were listed on the last page. The bottom corner listed a reminder to sign up for the summer book club, reading and discussing Ulrich Lehner's, *God is Not Nice*.

I couldn't have agreed more. God wasn't nice. As far as I knew, He betrayed me.

There were only two weeks before the book club began. The name of the group was deceiving. Our church club only met once, at the start of summer, to discuss afterthoughts of the book. Although I was thankful to find any distraction at the time, what I deemed a half-effort approach to a book club annoyed me.

I ordered the book online and it was on our doorstep in two days. From that time on, when I wasn't exercising with Dad, I was reading. As it turned out, while I agreed with Lehner about God not being nice, he pointed out what hadn't crossed my mind; why I wouldn't want Him to be. The book dove into society's perceptions of God being what reminded me of a genie. Tell God what I wanted and He'd grant my wish. I was in love with Drew. I wanted to spend the rest of my life with him, but my plans fell through. They fell through not because God was inferior or a liar, but because life happened. God knew every detail of my relationship with Drew. I thought my full potential would be met from a life with him, but to my surprise I was made for much, much more.

That summer I read book after book, learning God had a greater plan for my life than one I could imagine. I read the book of Ruth for the first time. In short, Naomi, who is a wife, mother, and follower of God, lost her husband and two sons. One of her sons' wives, Ruth who was devoted to Naomi, gets remarried and has a baby. In the last scene, Naomi rejoices in holding Ruth's baby; her new, sort-of grandson. That was it.

Why didn't all of Naomi's loved ones come back to life? How could she be content with a grand baby who wasn't technically hers? Naomi's son was supposed to be the father, not Ruth's new husband. Her humility, to love Ruth's baby despite losing her loved ones, sounded miserable. My stomach turned as I suspected this was the route my life would take, one requiring humility and finding joy in God's plan which would end up being nothing like my own. If anyone had to end up humble like Naomi, it would be me. As disappointing as it was, now that I knew of a better way to live, which would be for God, I couldn't ignore it.

After a summer of reading as many Christian books as I could, I longed to learn about Scripture the way I had been doing in chaplaincy school. In September, I joined the Scripture study group at church—which met on a weekly basis compared to the one-and-done summer book club. Other than the fast-paced lectures I partially absorbed in chaplaincy school, attending this group was my first time studying the Bible. I didn't count my childhood years of religious education as Bible study since I remembered nothing from it and spent the Bible time we did have, highlighting my best friends' names in whatever book we were reading. As a teen, I thought the Bible's contradictions showed its fallibility when in fact the discrepancies showed its Truth. Different authors of the Bible recorded events differently because of their unique vantage points; the results of the stories remained the same, over and over. I used to be bothered by the violence and suffering in the Bible. Since I couldn't make sense of the suffering, I ignored it. I missed the fact that, while God didn't want suffering for anyone, He still allowed it. Why would He allow suffering? When He created man He didn't want to be a puppeteer pulling on our strings at will and playing out our lives for us. He wanted us to make our own choice to love Him, or not. Thus, He gave up part of His strength so we,

His Creation, could have freedom of choice. A consequence of this freedom is suffering.

It was no wonder I took whatever I thought was the general, positive gist of the Bible to live by as a teen. The details were complicated and inconvenient. They demanded a death to my ego, a setting aside of my desires and opinions.

I was sitting at the long, brown lunch tables in the activity room at Scripture study, watching the weekly video lesson, when jealousy bubbled inside of me. The Scripture scholar pacing the TV screen talked of Jesus healing the sick. Specifically, the woman with a hemorrhage(Mark 5:25-34). I imagined myself in the passage. Rows of men stood between me and the dusty path Jesus was walking down. The men's sweaty backs clung to their thinning tunics. They were howling curses at Jesus while others praised his name, begging for healing as he walked past. I pushed through the stench of their bodies, to the edge of the path as Jesus walked by. I threw myself on the dusty ground and brushed the bottom tassel of his cloak. Suddenly, my arm and leg moved like normal. My spasticity was gone. My vision stilled and I could hear out of both ears. Jesus turned around at the feeling of his power leaving him. I ducked my head in fear of his reprimanding, but he knelt down and lifted my chin, saying my faith has saved me, to go in peace and be cured.

But I wasn't that woman. Why not? Why did she get to see Jesus and be healed, but I didn't?

Eventually, I came to know how close to Jesus I really was; how I was able to encounter Him every day. Beyond feeling Him in the warmth of the sun or the soulful music on my radio, I became one with God through the Eucharist, the body of Christ. What I used to see as a wafer and beg Dad for a bite of, as my seven-year-old self sat hungry in the pew during Mass, was healing me. Jesus would heal me in ways I didn't expect. Not as much in a concrete, physical way, but rather in a soulful way. From the inside out. The Eucharist was the closest I could get to Jesus here on earth.

In the years to follow, I continued to endure the constant shaking of my vision, the spasticity and high-tone on the left side of my body, hyper-nasal and slurred speech, decreased sensation, facial palsy, dysphagia, deafness in my right ear, minimal function of my left arm and leg, decreased balance, and drop foot. I still wore an AFO, alternated between using a cane and wheelchair to get around, endured stigma from strangers, and depended on Mom and Dad for transportation.

Nonetheless, I had a growing thankfulness. My deficits reminded me of my ultimate, inherent dependence on God not just physically, but spiritually. Apart from Him, I could do nothing. He was my very breath. Every step I took, I prayed for Jesus to walk with me and help me keep my balance. Before speaking, I prayed for Jesus to relieve the spasticity in my jaw. I daydreamed with Jesus, imagining my left arm reaching out before me. All of which kept me closer to Him than I ever could be, otherwise.

Since childhood, I had been on a hunt to find myself. I yearned for fame to complete me, to justify my value as a person. I tried to fit in with my peers by believing what they believed. I hoped a boyfriend would fill the void of my sense of purpose. I controlled my weight and eating in search of security. Even after my brain bleed, when I felt closest to God, I clung to my future plans with Drew.

When Drew ended our relationship, a path opened for me to build my life on God's unshakeable ground. On His foundation I wasn't limited to being Drew's Sweetheart. I was liberated as a sister of Christ, a beloved daughter of God, and a vessel through which His boundless Spirit could work.

To be sure, God would not Will anything destructive. In the same way He didn't want His son to have to suffer on the cross, He didn't want me to suffer an eating disorder, sexual shame, a brain bleed, physical disability, or rejection with years of heartache to follow. But He allowed it. I may not know the impact of my suffering since only God sees the big picture, but I can trust in its value. As St. Paul says, "We know that in all things God works for good with those who love Him" (Romans 8:28). Just as Christ's suffering redeemed the world, my suffering would serve its purpose, too.

God was unfolding a new plan for my life.

ACKNOWLEDGMENTS

F ATHER WISDOM, I'M not sure how to begin thanking you when I feel as overwhelmed with as much gratitude and humility as I do. How was I so blessed to have you join me on this journey? Your presence struck the match needed to light the fire in me to finish this book. Without you, the manuscript would still be half-finished, in a file on my computer. When I fell into the traps of distraction and self-doubt, you never ceased to pull me out with gentleness and love. Your mentorship has helped me grow deeper and more daring in my faith. I am eternally grateful for your guidance, friendship, and support. And this is just the beginning! Thank you.

Karen Schreck, you were a lamp to my feet as I started down this totally foreign path to writing a book. When I handed you my first draft, I thought I was handing you the Mona Lisa of all drafts; not out of pride but out of pure ignorance. Instead of criticizing my excessive use of Onomatopoeia and handful of run-on sentences, you targeted my strengths and showed me how to use them. In a world that puts limits, demands, and protocols on how a person should be, you taught me that in the art of writing, myself is the only way to be. Your patience and gentleness in our virtual classroom opens the way for others to thrive. You are attentive to the details of writing and of people. Thank you for teaching me the beauty of writing and being myself.

Mom & Dad, living out this story one time was enough. Yet, you willingly re-lived it, helping to edit, until I felt the draft was finished. Thank you for being the selfless, loving, supportive parents you are and for trusting in God's plan.

Tom, I am blessed to have you as my brother. I know you're the better writer, but I hope this book makes you proud. Thank you for your guidance throughout this journey and encouraging me to stick with it. Love you.

Mary Beth Lang, you may never realize how generous and impactful your help was on this journey. From conversations about basic editing to life trials, your support moved my heart and the progress of this book. Thank you.

Nathaniel & Mary Gee, your unwavering support, prayers, and friendship were crucial to the completion of this book. You humbly connected me with Father Wisdom, opening the way for God to work. Your discipleship inspires me and brings me closer to Jesus. I hope to never stop learning from you. Thank you for your love.

Heather Ann Martinez, I was anxious about sharing the faith-side and before-and-after material of my brain bleed with our group. I feared how vulnerable of a position it would put me in and how the added parts would be received. When Karen finished reading my piece, your face was beaming. You were ectatic that I was sharing my faith and more of my life because I am not my diagnosis. Your support helped build my confidence and motivation to be bold. You patiently answered my slew of last-minute questions and eased my insecurities. Thank you.

Kevin Daly, Nathaniel & Mary Gee, Danielle Bruner, & Casey Bonesso, thank you for graciously giving your time and feedback throughout the many drafts of this book. Your confidence in me fueled my growth and courage to keep writing. Thank you.

Kathleen Stear & Dr. Terry Schlabach, God was at work through the two of you. Thank you for inspiring me to share my story and thank you for believing in me.

Caring Bridge readers (family and friends), you have rallied behind me since the day I awoke post surgery. Who knew Mom's blog would turn into this? Your ongoing prayers and fierce support have been critical to my recovery. Thank you and Happy Sunday.

JENNIFER KRAY IS a first-time author and seasoned public speaker. She received Honorable Mention in the 91st Annual *Writer's Digest* Writing Competition in 2022. Over the years, she has had the privilege of sharing her patient experience with several institutions such as Loyola University Medical Center, Silvercross Hospital, and her alma mater, St. Ambrose University.

She continues to write on the blog her mother started the day after her brainstem hemorrhage to update family and friends on her recovery. Kray writes about the challenges and progress she has made, as well as the spiritual wisdom which has emanated from it. When she isn't writing, she likes to be outside working in her adaptive garden, spending time in prayer, or trying to train her free-spirited Great Dane named Toula.

Printed in Great Britain
by Amazon

20440840R00139